MUTSUMI MASUDA, C.B. CEBULSKI AND **KIA ASAMIYA**
Translation and Adaptation

LAURA JACKSON AND **YOKO KOBAYASHI**
Additional Translation

DAN NAKROSIS AND **DANO INK STUDIOS**
Retouch and Lettering

VERONICA CASSON
Cover Designer

VANESSA SATONE
Designer

STEPHEN PAKULA
Production Supervisor

MIKE LACKEY
Print Production Manager

STEPHANIE SHALOFSKY
Vice President, Production

JOHN O'DONNELL
Publisher

Special thanks to Mitsuru Uehira

World Peace Through Shared Popular Culture™
centralparkmedia.com
cpmmanga.com

Dark Angel Book One. Published by CPM Manga, a division of Central Park Media Corporation. Office of Publication – 250 West 57th Street, Suite 317, New York, NY 10107. Original Japanese Version "DARK ANGEL, Volume 1" © KIA ASAMIYA 1992. Originally published in Japan in 1992 by KADOKAWA SHOTEN PUBLISHING Co., Ltd., TOKYO. English version ©2000 Central Park Media Corporation. CPM Manga and logo are registered trademarks of Central Park Media Corporation. All rights reserved. Price per copy $9.99, price in Canada may vary. ISBN: 1-58664-899-3. Catalog number: CMX 62301MM. UPC: 7-19987-00623-2-48993. Printed in Canada.

DARK ANGEL

BOOK ONE

KIA ASAMIYA
Writer and Artist

CPM ®
MANGA

w York, New York

CONTENTS

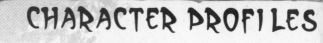

CHARACTER PROFILES

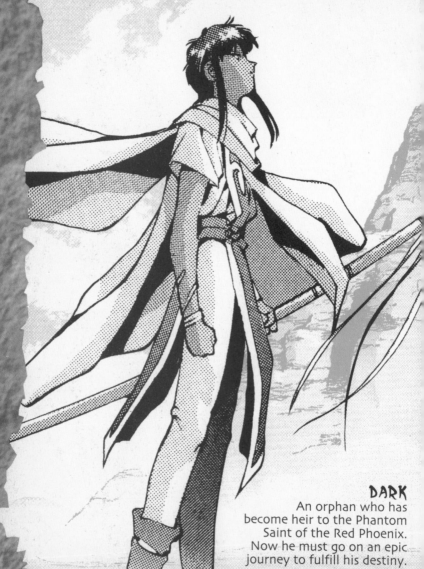

DARK
An orphan who has become heir to the Phantom Saint of the Red Phoenix. Now he must go on an epic journey to fulfill his destiny.

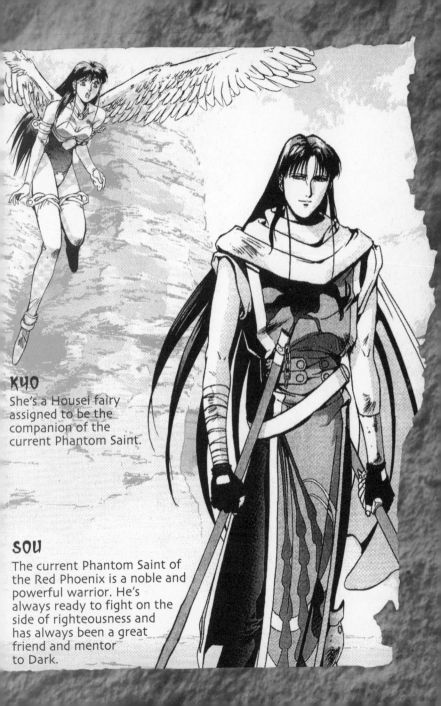

KYO

She's a Housei fairy assigned to be the companion of the current Phantom Saint.

SOU

The current Phantom Saint of the Red Phoenix is a noble and powerful warrior. He's always ready to fight on the side of righteousness and has always been a great friend and mentor to Dark.

Push on courageously...
Dark Angel is in the world.

The four
countries
surrounding
Oukoku are
ruled by the
Phantom
Saints.

DARK ANGEL

IN THAT WORLD, THERE ARE INDEED MANY WANDERERS.
THERE ARE INDEED MANY LIVES AND MANY DEATHS.
THERE ARE MANY DIFFERENT FORMS OF EXISTENCE.
BUT ULTIMATELY, MAN LIVES AND DIES BY THE SWORD.

HOWEVER, THERE IS ONE. AND WHAT OF HIS APPEARANCE?
ON WINGS DYED AS IF WITH VERMILLION,
THE WINDS CARRY HIM THROUGH THE SKIES.
WITH BLACK BLOOD BEATING IN HIS HEART, HE RISES FROM THE EARTH.
WITH EYES BLUE AS THE SKY, HE SURVEYS THE LANDS AROUND HIM.

THIS BODY...
IS SAVAGE AND UNTAMED.
ONE FACE IS THAT OF THE PROTECTOR.
BUT AS IN EVERY OTHER WORLD,
THE OTHER FACE IS THAT OF...

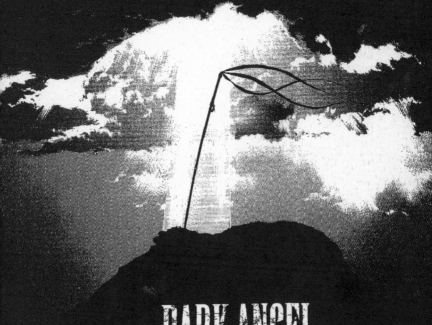

DARK ANGEL

HIIIYAAAH!

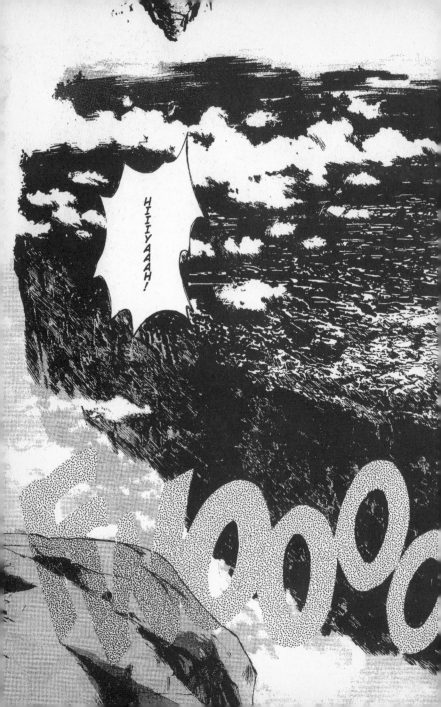

HAAIIIIII!

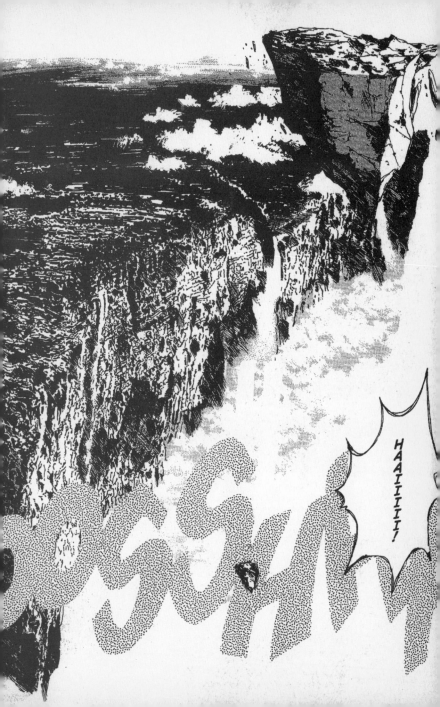

KTCHINK
TOK
WHAT?!
HEH!

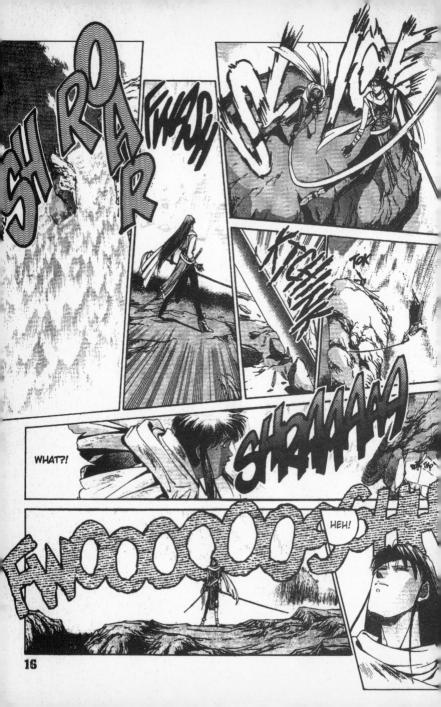

YAAAAHH!
...
SPLASH!
HUH?!

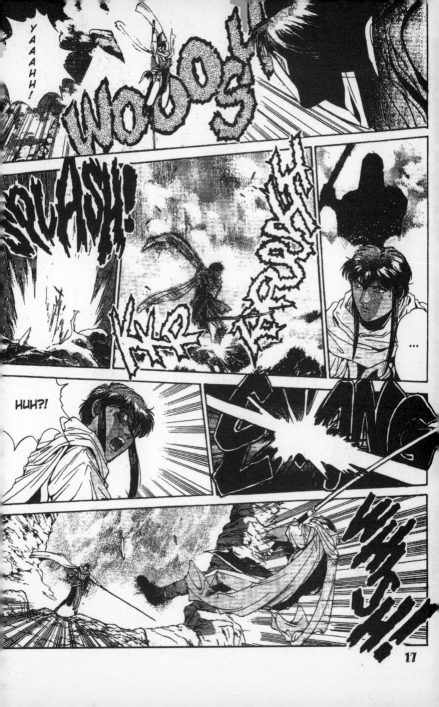

!!
THUD
YOU'RE STILL LETTING YOUR SWORD SWING YOU.
WHAT'S WRONG, DARK?
Y... YES. I'M SORRY.
puff...
huff...
...
huff...

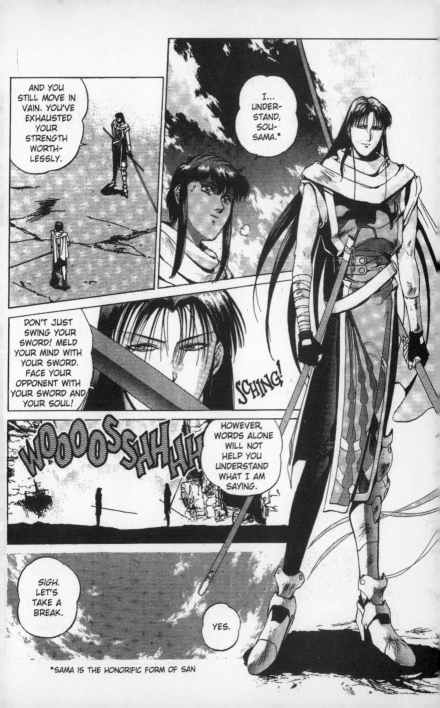

AND YOU STILL MOVE IN VAIN. YOU'VE EXHAUSTED YOUR STRENGTH WORTHLESSLY.

I... UNDERSTAND, SOU-SAMA.*

DON'T JUST SWING YOUR SWORD! MELD YOUR MIND WITH YOUR SWORD. FACE YOUR OPPONENT WITH YOUR SWORD AND YOUR SOUL!

SCHING!

WOOOOSSHHHHH

HOWEVER, WORDS ALONE WILL NOT HELP YOU UNDERSTAND WHAT I AM SAYING.

SIGH. LET'S TAKE A BREAK.

YES.

*SAMA IS THE HONORIFIC FORM OF SAN

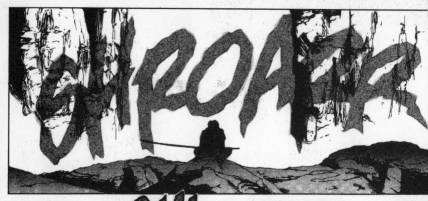

SHROAK

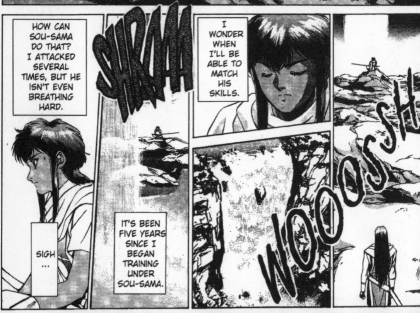

HOW CAN SOU-SAMA DO THAT? I ATTACKED SEVERAL TIMES, BUT HE ISN'T EVEN BREATHING HARD.

SHRAAA

I WONDER WHEN I'LL BE ABLE TO MATCH HIS SKILLS.

SIGH...

IT'S BEEN FIVE YEARS SINCE I BEGAN TRAINING UNDER SOU-SAMA.

WOOOSSH

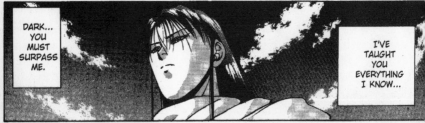

DARK... YOU MUST SURPASS ME.

I'VE TAUGHT YOU EVERYTHING I KNOW...

20

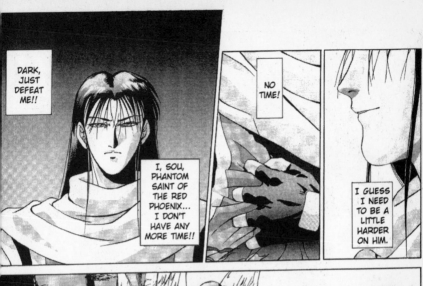

DARK, JUST DEFEAT ME!!

I, SOU, PHANTOM SAINT OF THE RED PHOENIX... I DON'T HAVE ANY MORE TIME!!

NO TIME!

I GUESS I NEED TO BE A LITTLE HARDER ON HIM.

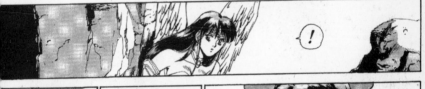

DARK!!

YOU'VE GOT YOUR BREATH BACK NOW!! THIS IS YOUR LAST LESSON! I'VE TRAINED YOU FOR OVER FIVE YEARS NOW. IF YOU CAN'T DEFEAT ME--

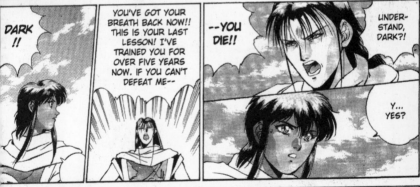

--YOU DIE!!

UNDERSTAND, DARK?!

Y... YES?

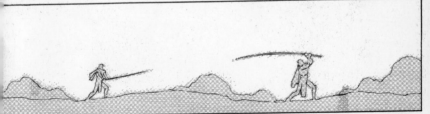

WHISH
UUGH!
ULP!

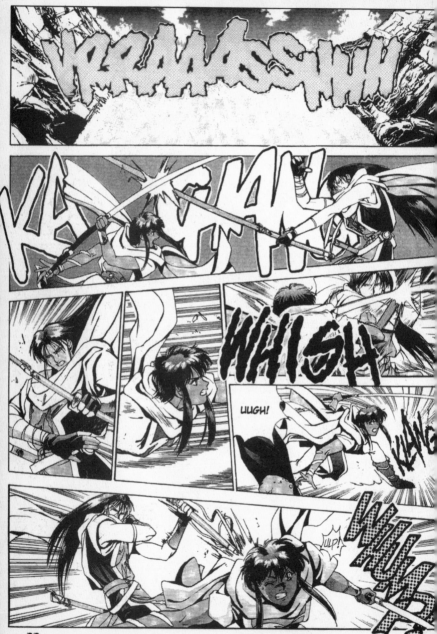

NOT--
KLANG
--YET!!
HUH?
WHOOSH
SMAK!
HUFF
HUFF
HUFF
HUFF
HUFF
KATCHINK
SUUUUUU!
HMM...
SLICE

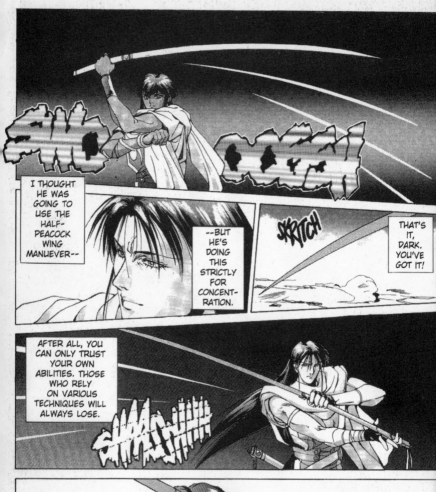

I THOUGHT HE WAS GOING TO USE THE HALF-PEACOCK WING MANUEVER--

--BUT HE'S DOING THIS STRICTLY FOR CONCENTRATION.

SKRITCH

THAT'S IT, DARK. YOU'VE GOT IT!

AFTER ALL, YOU CAN ONLY TRUST YOUR OWN ABILITIES. THOSE WHO RELY ON VARIOUS TECHNIQUES WILL ALWAYS LOSE.

SHHASHHH

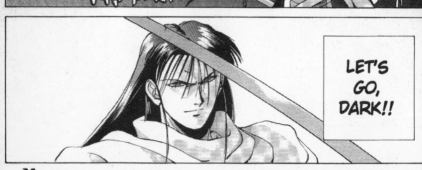

LET'S GO, DARK!!

OH, MIGHTY PEACOCK, THROUGH ILLUSIONS OF LIGHT AND WATER, GUIDE MY KILLING BLOW!!
SWOOOSH
HIIIYAAAAH!

SLICE
SPRAAASHH
HE CUT THE WATER-FALL!!
HE'S GREAT.
HIS SCAB-BARD?!
DARK IS--
--ABOVE ME?!

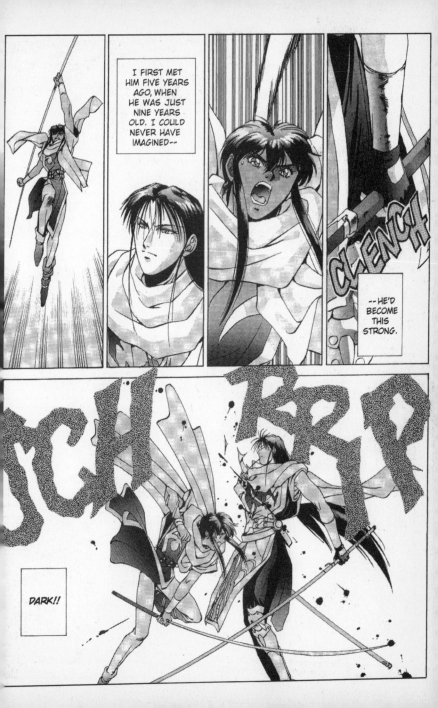

I FIRST MET HIM FIVE YEARS AGO, WHEN HE WAS JUST NINE YEARS OLD. I COULD NEVER HAVE IMAGINED--

CLENCH

--HE'D BECOME THIS STRONG.

DARK!!

SOU-SAMA!!
TOK
SOU-SAMA!!
SOU-SAMA, WHY DID YOU LOWER YOUR SWORD!?
YOU COULD HAVE DODGED OR BLOCKED IT IF YOU WANTED TO! AND WHY DIDN'T YOU CHANGE FORMS?!
UUGH... DARK, MY SWORD WOULD HAVE BEEN WORTHLESS AGAINST YOU...
AND YOU DIDN'T CHANGE FORMS EITHER.
DARK, YOU'RE READY NOW. YOU'VE PROVEN YOURSELF. THERE WAS NOTHING MORE I COULD TEACH YOU. YOU ARE THE NEXT PHANTOM SAINT OF THE RED PHOENIX.
DARK, YOU ARE FULLY PRE-PARED!!
SOU-SAMA!
HA HA HA... MY LIFE IS NEARLY OVER. BUT NOW, BEFORE I DIE--
--I'M ABLE TO LOOK UPON THE FACE OF THE NEXT PHANTOM SAINT.
DARK, GO TO OUKOKU AND DECLARE YOURSELF THE NEW PHANTOM SAINT OF THE RED PHOENIX!!

GOOD-BYE, DARK...
DARK, YOU UNDERSTAND. THIS IS YOURS NOW. THE SWORD OF THE RED PHOENIX, IT PROVES YOU ARE THE PHANTOM SAINT.
FWOOSH
SOU-SAMA!!

SOU-
SAMA
!!
WOOOOOSH

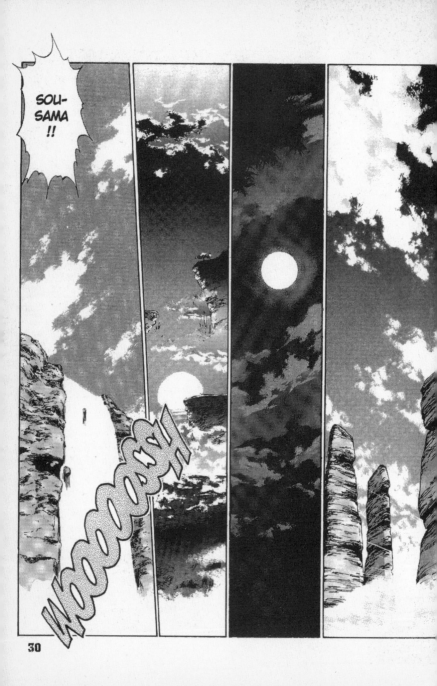

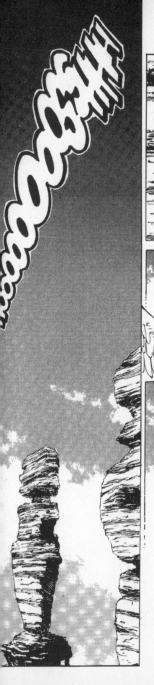

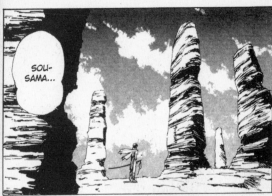

SOU-SAMA...

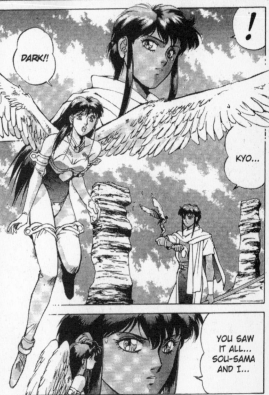

DARK!!

!

KYO...

YOU SAW IT ALL... SOU-SAMA AND I...

31

DARK, IT WASN'T YOUR FAULT!!
IT'S NO ONE'S FAULT.
KYO...
I BELIEVE THIS IS WHAT SOU-SAMA WANTED.
SOU-SAMA WANTED *THIS?*
IT WAS SOU-SAMA'S TIME.
AS A PHANTOM SAINT, SOU-SAMA WANTED ETERNAL SLEEP TO COME BY YOUR HAND.
I GUESS HE KNEW HIS TIME HAD COME AND WANTED TO GO OUT FIGHTING.
I'VE HEARD SOU-SAMA BECAME A PHANTOM SAINT ALMOST THE SAME WAY.
!
KYO, THE ONLY THING LEFT FOR ME TO DO IS KEEP MY PROMISE TO SOU-SAMA.
THAT'S WHAT I THINK.
TOK
DARK, WAIT!! I'M COMING TOO!!

I'M GOING!! I'M GOING TO OUKOKU!!

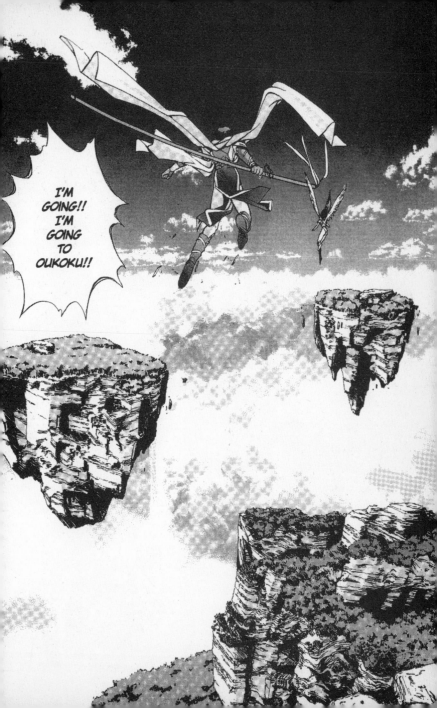

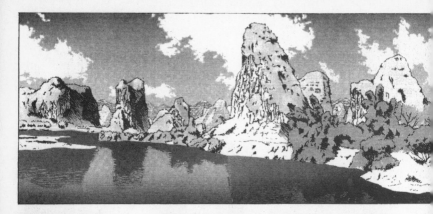

BLUE DRAGON HALL.

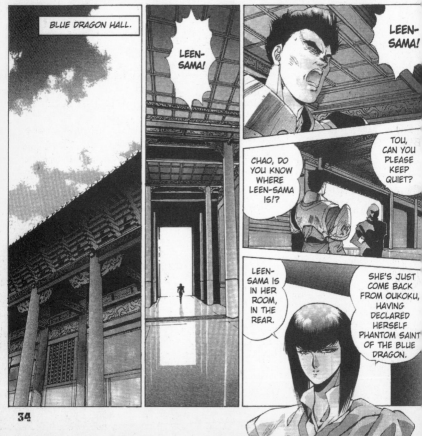

LEEN-SAMA!

LEEN-SAMA!

CHAO, DO YOU KNOW WHERE LEEN-SAMA IS!?

TOU, CAN YOU PLEASE KEEP QUIET?

LEEN-SAMA IS IN HER ROOM, IN THE REAR.

SHE'S JUST COME BACK FROM OUKOKU, HAVING DECLARED HERSELF PHANTOM SAINT OF THE BLUE DRAGON.

YOU SHOULD EXCUSE YOURSELF AND STOP BOTHERING LEEN-SAMA.
B... BUT...
IS SOME-THING WRONG, TOU?
I'D BE HAPPY TO LISTEN.
THE TRUTH IS, SOMEONE HAS WANDERED INTO TOI. WHAT'S MORE, THEY'RE FROM NANBAN.
WHAT?!
THAT'S ODD. THEY'RE VIOLATING THE TREATY BETWEEN THE TERRITORIES OF THE FOUR WINDS.
WE'RE SUPPOSED TO GET NOTICE BEFORE THEY ENTER.
THE RULER OF NANBAN, SOU-SAMA, PHANTOM SAINT OF THE RED PHOENIX, IS USUALLY VERY STRICT ABOUT COURTESY.
THERE MIGHT BE SOMETHING HAPPENING IN NANBAN OR SOME-THING MAY BE WRONG WITH THE PHANTOM SAINT OF THE RED PHOENIX.
HMM...
ALL RIGHT!! WHY DON'T WE GO AND CHECK INTO THIS?!
YEAH!
WAIT!

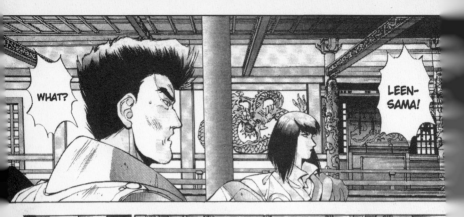

WHAT?

LEEN-SAMA!

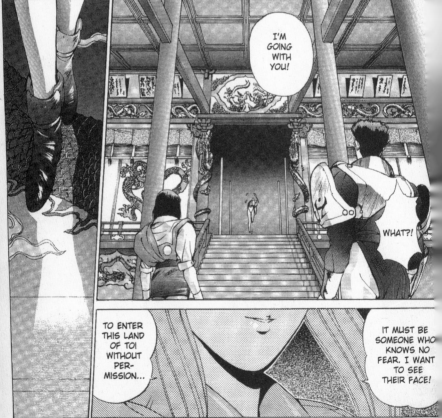

I'M GOING WITH YOU!

WHAT?!

TO ENTER THIS LAND OF TOI WITHOUT PER-MISSION...

IT MUST BE SOMEONE WHO KNOWS NO FEAR. I WANT TO SEE THEIR FACE!

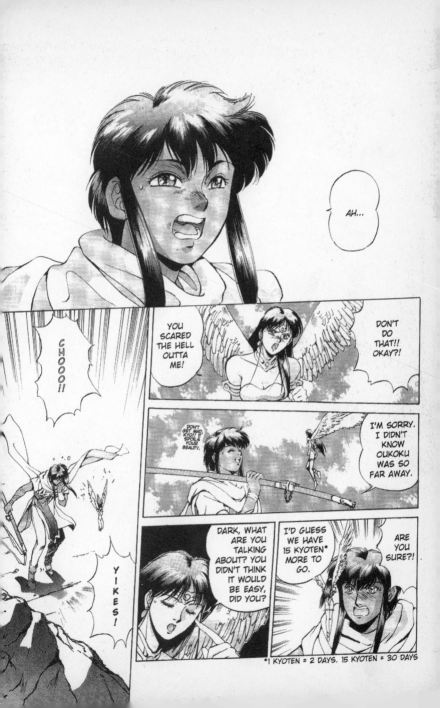

*1 KYOTEN = 2 DAYS. 15 KYOTEN = 30 DAYS

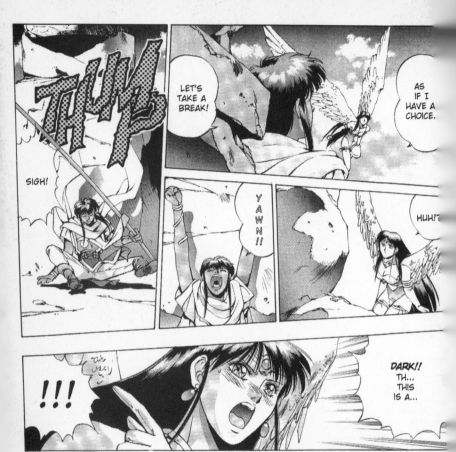

THUMP

LET'S TAKE A BREAK!

AS IF I HAVE A CHOICE.

SIGH!

YAWN!!

HUH!?

!!!

DARK!! TH... THIS IS A...

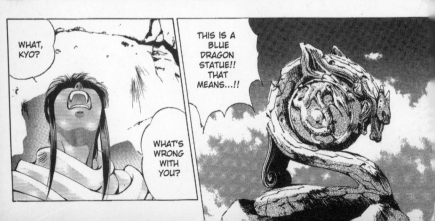

WHAT, KYO?

THIS IS A BLUE DRAGON STATUE!! THAT MEANS...!!

WHAT'S WRONG WITH YOU?

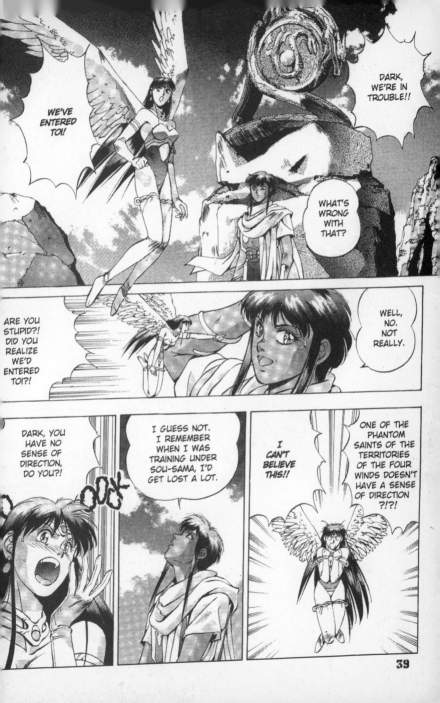

DARK, WE'RE IN TROUBLE!!

WE'VE ENTERED TOI!

WHAT'S WRONG WITH THAT?

ARE YOU STUPID?! DID YOU REALIZE WE'D ENTERED TOI?!

WELL, NO. NOT REALLY.

DARK, YOU HAVE NO SENSE OF DIRECTION, DO YOU?!

OOCK

I GUESS NOT. I REMEMBER WHEN I WAS TRAINING UNDER SOU-SAMA, I'D GET LOST A LOT.

I CAN'T BELIEVE THIS!!

ONE OF THE PHANTOM SAINTS OF THE TERRITORIES OF THE FOUR WINDS DOESN'T HAVE A SENSE OF DIRECTION ?!?!

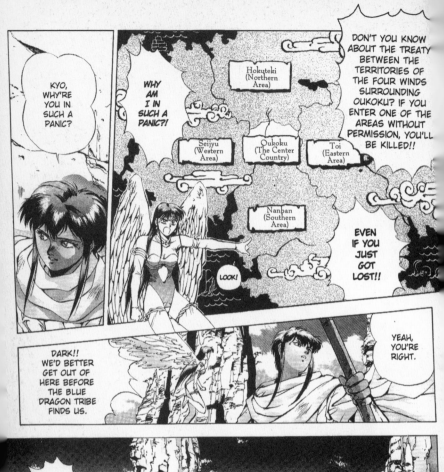

KYO, WHY'RE YOU IN SUCH A PANIC?

WHY AM I IN SUCH A PANIC?!

DON'T YOU KNOW ABOUT THE TREATY BETWEEN THE TERRITORIES OF THE FOUR WINDS SURROUNDING OUKOKU? IF YOU ENTER ONE OF THE AREAS WITHOUT PERMISSION, YOU'LL BE KILLED!!

Hokuteki (Northern Area)

Seijyu (Western Area)

Oukoku (The Center Country)

Toi (Eastern Area)

Nanban (Southern Area)

LOOK!

EVEN IF YOU JUST GOT LOST!!

DARK!! WE'D BETTER GET OUT OF HERE BEFORE THE BLUE DRAGON TRIBE FINDS US.

YEAH, YOU'RE RIGHT.

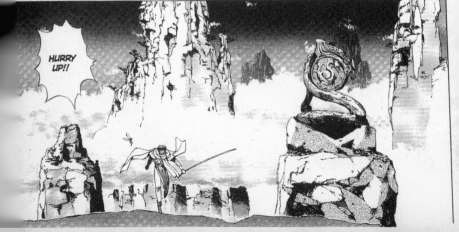

HURRY UP!!

HEY, KYO, I THINK WE'RE BACK IN NANBAN NOW...
PUFF
PUFF
PUFF
WELL...
!!
W... WHAT?!
IN THE MOUNTAIN... AN ENORMOUS CARVING OF A BLUE DRAGON.
THAT MEANS ...

WHAT!?
YOU REALLY ARE GOOD FOR NOTHING!!
OH, NO!! DARK, WE'RE IN THE MIDDLE OF TOI!!
YOU IDIOT!
LOOK OUT!!
KABOOOOM
WHOOOOSH
WHO... WHO'S THERE?!

I AM LEEN!!
I AM ONE OF THE FOUR PHANTOM SAINTS... FROM THE BLUE DRAGON KINGDON.

YOU OF THE RED PHOENIX!
WHY HAVE YOU COME INTO THE BLUE DRAGON KINGDOM WITHOUT PERMISSION!?!
OH, NO. THIS IS WHAT I WAS AFRAID OF.
WHAT SHOULD WE DO?
WOOOOOSSHH
PHANTOM SAINT OF THE BLUE DRAGON ...LEEN?

SHE'S THE PHANTOM SAINT--
--OF THE BLUE DRAGON?!
TOK
!
!!
SPOK

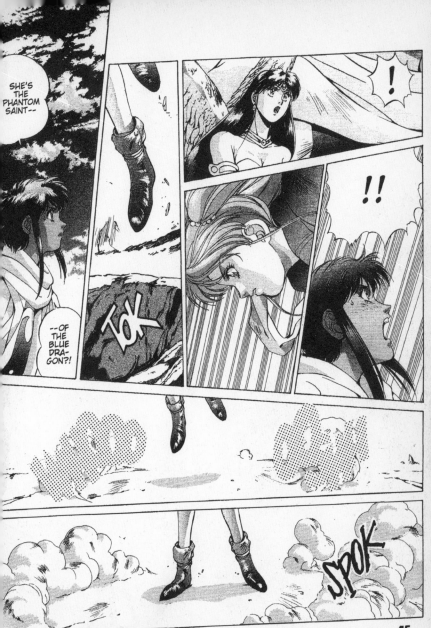

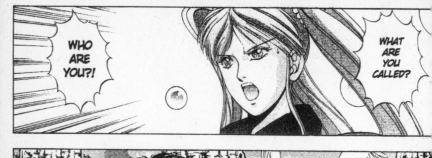

WHO ARE YOU?!

WHAT ARE YOU CALLED?

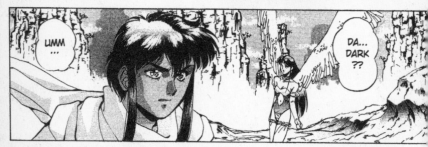

LIMM...

DA... DARK ??

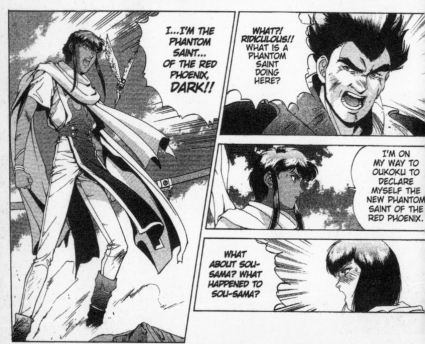

I...I'M THE PHANTOM SAINT... OF THE RED PHOENIX, DARK!!

WHAT?! RIDICULOUS!! WHAT IS A PHANTOM SAINT DOING HERE?

I'M ON MY WAY TO OUKOKU TO DECLARE MYSELF THE NEW PHANTOM SAINT OF THE RED PHOENIX.

WHAT ABOUT SOLI-SAMA? WHAT HAPPENED TO SOLI-SAMA?

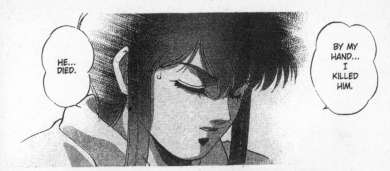

HE... DIED.

BY MY HAND... I KILLED HIM.

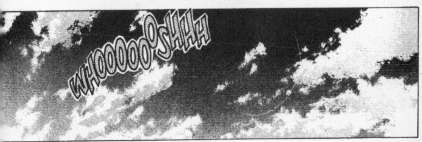

WHOOOOOOSHHH

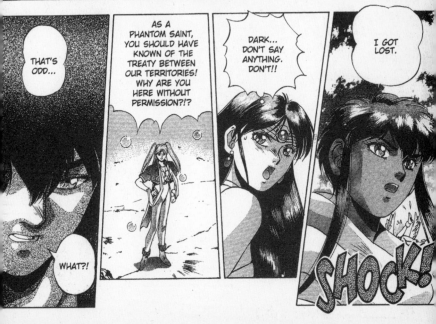

THAT'S ODD...

AS A PHANTOM SAINT, YOU SHOULD HAVE KNOWN OF THE TREATY BETWEEN OUR TERRITORIES! WHY ARE YOU HERE WITHOUT PERMISSION?!?

DARK... DON'T SAY ANYTHING. DON'T!!

I GOT LOST.

WHAT?!

SHOCK!

WHAT?
WHY DIDN'T YOU LISTEN TO ME?
OH, NO.
HAHAHAHAHAHA HAHAHA!
?
YOUR IGNORANCE HAS BEEN BROUGHT TO LIGHT.
WH... WHAT'S SO FUNNY!?
GGGRRRR

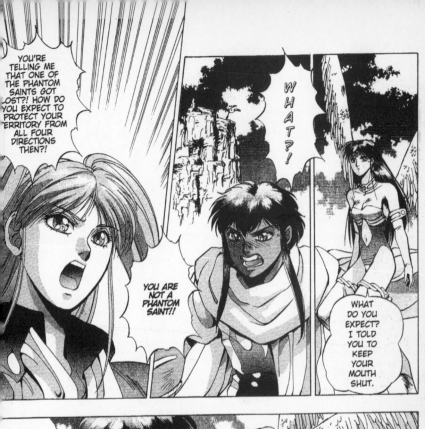

YOU'RE TELLING ME THAT ONE OF THE PHANTOM SAINTS GOT LOST?! HOW DO YOU EXPECT TO PROTECT YOUR TERRITORY FROM ALL FOUR DIRECTIONS THEN?!

WHAT?!

YOU ARE NOT A PHANTOM SAINT!!

WHAT DO YOU EXPECT? I TOLD YOU TO KEEP YOUR MOUTH SHUT.

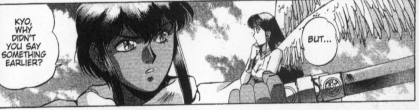

KYO, WHY DIDN'T YOU SAY SOMETHING EARLIER?

BUT...

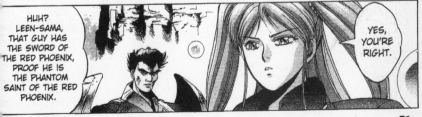

HUH? LEEN-SAMA, THAT GUY HAS THE SWORD OF THE RED PHOENIX, PROOF HE IS THE PHANTOM SAINT OF THE RED PHOENIX.

YES, YOU'RE RIGHT.

51

YET, I STILL CAN'T BELIEVE IT.
WHAT DID YOU SAY!?
LEEN-SAMA, LET ME TEST THIS CHILD'S POWER.
FINE.
THEY'RE GOING TO ATTACK.
BE CAREFUL, DARK!!
I AM TOU, OF THE BLUE DRAGON KINGDOM, OF THE HOUSE OF TACHIUO.
HOOOOOH
NOW, LET'S SEE IF YOU REALLY ARE THE PHANTOM SAINT OF THE RED PHOENIX!!
WWWWW

CLIK
CLIK
IT SEEMS NO MATTER WHAT I SAY, YOU WON'T BELIEVE ME...
WHWHOOOOSSH
FWOOOM
HOW IS HE GOING TO FIGHT WITH ME WITH THOSE?
WHAT?! HIS SWORDS HAVE NO BLADES!
KA-CHAK!

WHOOOSHH
MY SWORD WILL CUT YOU LIKE A FISH SLICING THROUGH WATER!!
CA
CHANG
HEH!
TOK
WHAT?! THE SWORD OF THE RED PHOENIX'S CHAIN WON'T RELEASE!!
SNEER

KTCHINK
WAAHHH!
HAAAIIIII!
STMP

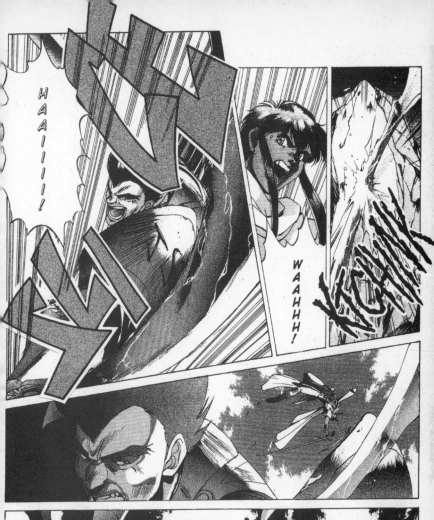

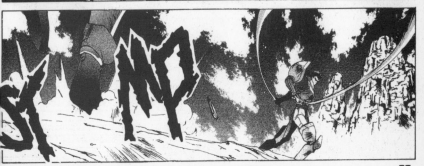

!
D...
THE ROCKS! THE WATER IS REALLY THAT POWERFUL?!
KRAK
I GUESS HE'S PRETTY NIMBLE.
WHAT?
HUH?!
KWOOOOOSH
NEXT TIME, CLOTHING WON'T BE THE ONLY THING MY SWORD CUTS.
DAMN!

HERE'S A SECRET TECHNIQUE! TWISTING SWORDS STRIKE SWIFTY!

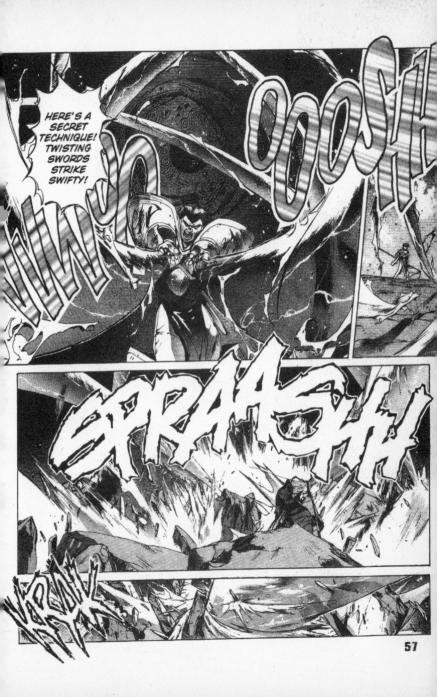

SPLAASHHH
FOR DARIN TO DECEIVE US ABOUT BEING A PHANTOM SAINT, I GRANT YOU DEATH!!
THERE'S NO WAY TO DODGE IT, NO MATTER HOW AGILE YOU ARE!!
FWISH
HEH HEH. WELL, THAT SETTLES THAT.
YES.
HA HA HA HA HA!
THAT ATTACK SLICES THROUGH SOLID GROUND WITH JETS OF WATER!
SPLOSHH
!
SPWASH

GASP!
WHAT!? YOU... YOU WERE... INSIDE MY WATER?!
IM-POSS-IBLE!!
I'M IMPRESSED. THAT SWORD OF YOURS CUTS WELL.
HOWEVER, IF I MOVE WITH THE WATER, IT'S POSSIBLE TO STAY OUT OF HARM'S WAY...
BESIDES, EVER SINCE I WAS A CHILD--
--I'VE BEEN A GOOD SWIMMER.

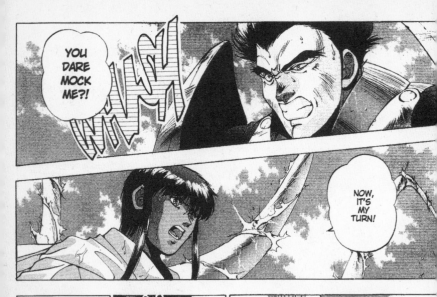

YOU DARE MOCK ME?!

NOW, IT'S MY TURN!

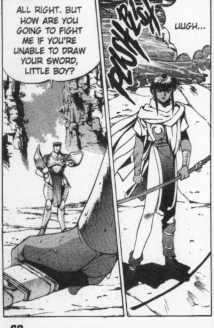

ALL RIGHT. BUT HOW ARE YOU GOING TO FIGHT ME IF YOU'RE UNABLE TO DRAW YOUR SWORD, LITTLE BOY?

UUGH...

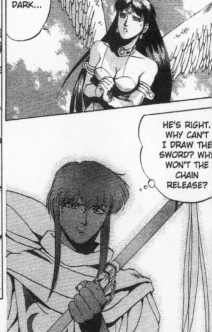

DARK...

HE'S RIGHT. WHY CAN'T I DRAW THE SWORD? WHY WON'T THE CHAIN RELEASE?

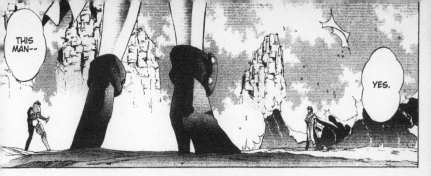

THIS MAN--

YES.

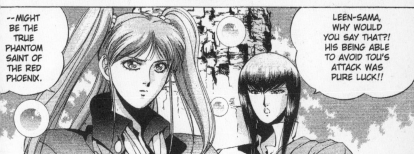

--MIGHT BE THE TRUE PHANTOM SAINT OF THE RED PHOENIX.

LEEN-SAMA, WHY WOULD YOU SAY THAT?! HIS BEING ABLE TO AVOID TOU'S ATTACK WAS PURE LUCK!!

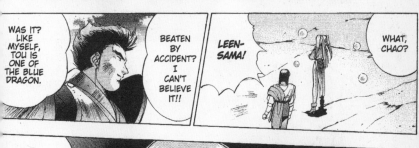

WAS IT? LIKE MYSELF, TOU IS ONE OF THE BLUE DRAGON.

BEATEN BY ACCIDENT? I CAN'T BELIEVE IT!!

LEEN-SAMA!

WHAT, CHAO?

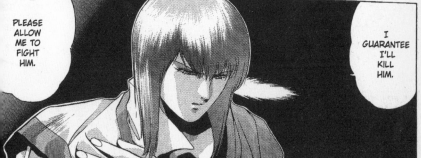

PLEASE ALLOW ME TO FIGHT HIM.

I GUARANTEE I'LL KILL HIM.

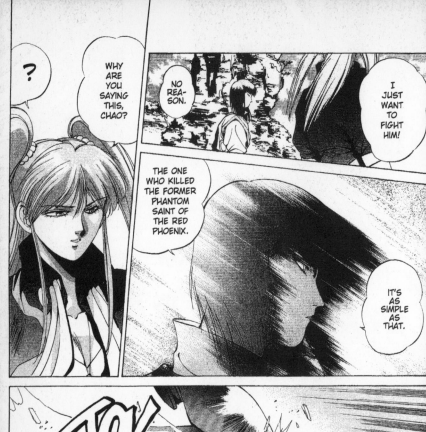

WHY ARE YOU SAYING THIS, CHAO?

?

NO REA- SON.

I JUST WANT TO FIGHT HIM!

THE ONE WHO KILLED THE FORMER PHANTOM SAINT OF THE RED PHOENIX.

IT'S AS SIMPLE AS THAT.

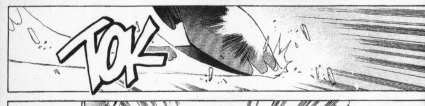

TOK

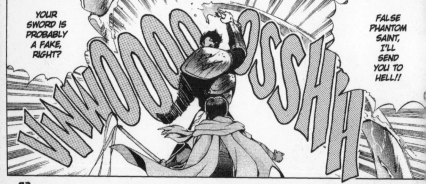

YOUR SWORD IS PROBABLY A FAKE, RIGHT?

UWOOOOOOSSHH

FALSE PHANTOM SAINT, I'LL SEND YOU TO HELL!!

WHOOOOOOOOOOSHHHH
LET THE HEAVENS RAIN AND FORM A SPHERE OF WATER!
RAAARRGG!

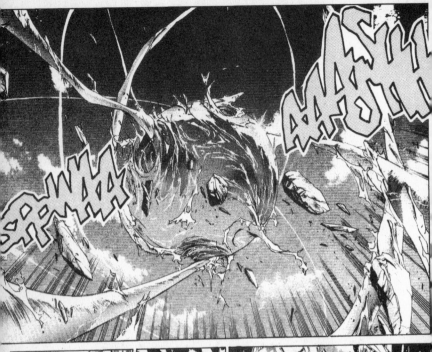

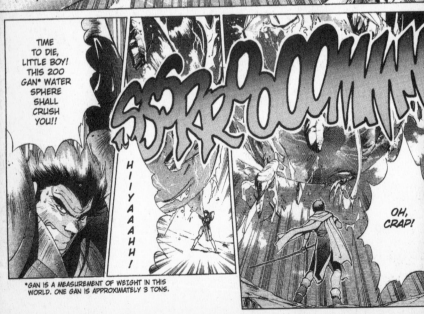

TIME TO DIE, LITTLE BOY! THIS 200 GAN* WATER SPHERE SHALL CRUSH YOU!!

HIIYAAAHH!

OH, CRAP!

*GAN IS A MEASUREMENT OF WEIGHT IN THIS WORLD. ONE GAN IS APPROXIMATELY 3 TONS.

NNOOOOOO!
DARK!
CHAO, I GUESS YOU WON'T GET YOUR TURN AFTER ALL.
SO BE IT.
KAGOOM!
UH-OH!

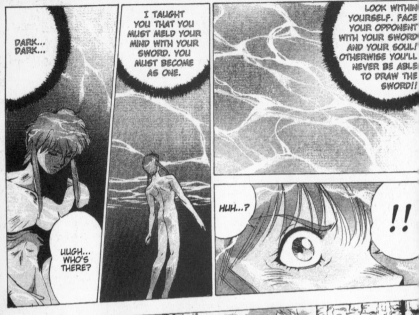

DARK... DARK...

I TAUGHT YOU THAT YOU MUST MELD YOUR MIND WITH YOUR SWORD. YOU MUST BECOME AS ONE.

LOOK WITHIN YOURSELF. FACE YOUR OPPONENT WITH YOUR SWORD AND YOUR SOUL! OTHERWISE YOU'LL NEVER BE ABLE TO DRAW THE SWORD!!

UUGH... WHO'S THERE?

HUH...?

!!

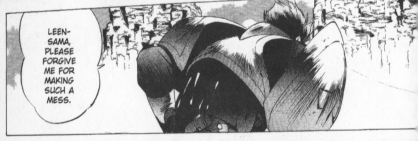

LEEN-SAMA, PLEASE FORGIVE ME FOR MAKING SUCH A MESS.

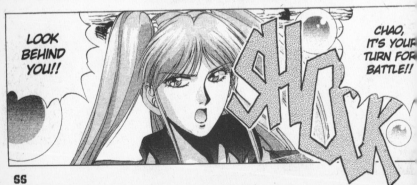

LOOK BEHIND YOU!!

SHOCK

CHAO, IT'S YOUR TURN FOR BATTLE!!

AAHHH...
DARK!!
DARK!!
HEH! THAT'S THE END OF HIM.
RUMBLE
TOU, WHAT ARE YOU TAKING ABOUT?
I HAVE NOW BROUGHT AN END TO THIS.
!!
WHAT?!

OOOSH!!!

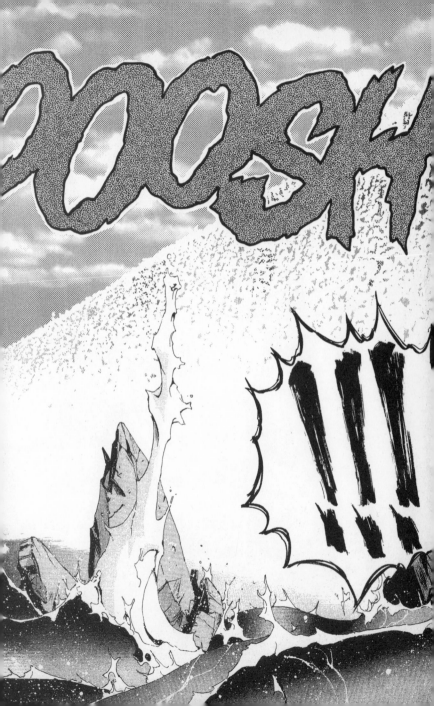

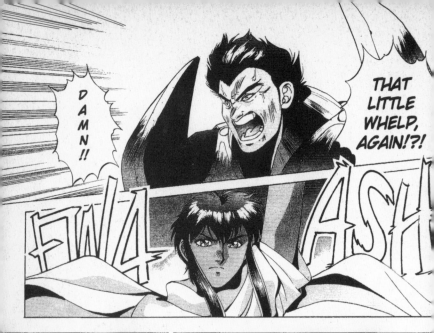

DAMN!!

THAT LITTLE WHELP, AGAIN!?!

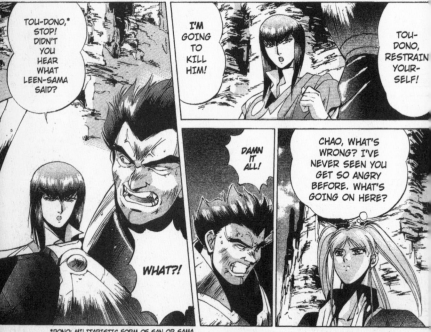

TOLI-DONO,* STOP! DIDN'T YOU HEAR WHAT LEEN-SAMA SAID?

I'M GOING TO KILL HIM!

TOU-DONO, RESTRAIN YOURSELF!

DAMN IT ALL!

CHAO, WHAT'S WRONG? I'VE NEVER SEEN YOU GET SO ANGRY BEFORE. WHAT'S GOING ON HERE?

WHAT?!

*DONO: MILITARISTIC FORM OF SAN OR SAMA

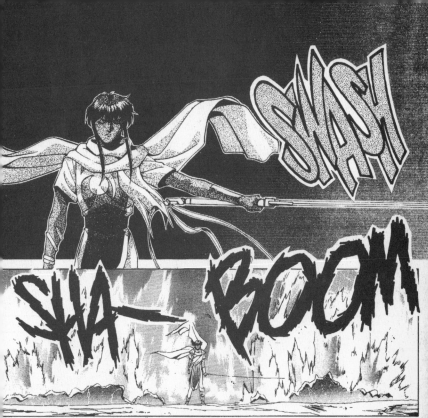

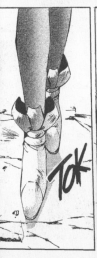

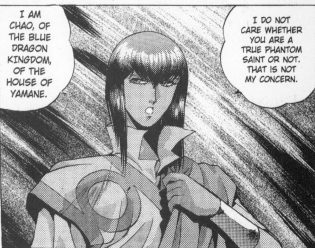

I AM CHAO, OF THE BLUE DRAGON KINGDOM, OF THE HOUSE OF YAMANE.

I DO NOT CARE WHETHER YOU ARE A TRUE PHANTOM SAINT OR NOT. THAT IS NOT MY CONCERN.

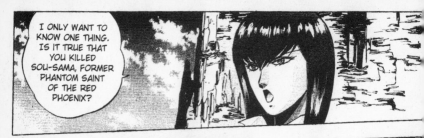

I ONLY WANT TO KNOW ONE THING. IS IT TRUE THAT YOU KILLED SOU-SAMA, FORMER PHANTOM SAINT OF THE RED PHOENIX?

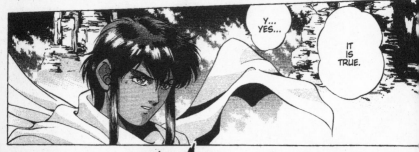

Y... YES...

IT IS TRUE.

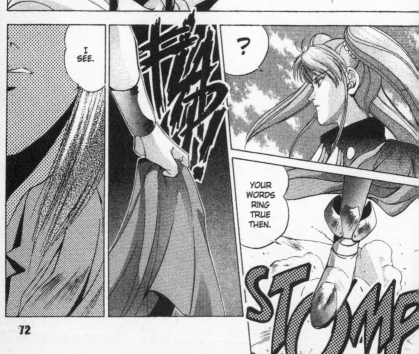

I SEE.

?

YOUR WORDS RING TRUE THEN.

72

WOOOSHH
I AM GOING TO KILL YOU, ENEMY OF SOU-SAMA.
YOU ARE MINE, DARK!!
ENEMY?
SHE BELIEVES I WAS SOU-SAMA'S ENEMY!?

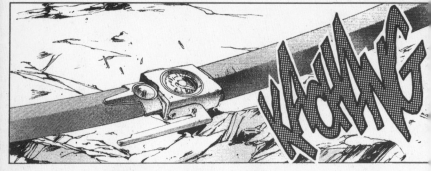

KA-CHING

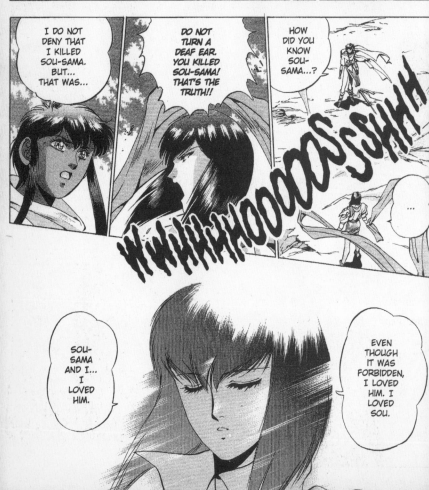

I DO NOT DENY THAT I KILLED SOU-SAMA. BUT... THAT WAS...

DO NOT TURN A DEAF EAR. YOU KILLED SOU-SAMA! THAT'S THE TRUTH!!

HOW DID YOU KNOW SOU-SAMA...?

WHHHHHHOOOOOSSHHH

...

SOU-SAMA AND I... I LOVED HIM.

EVEN THOUGH IT WAS FORBIDDEN, I LOVED HIM. I LOVED SOU.

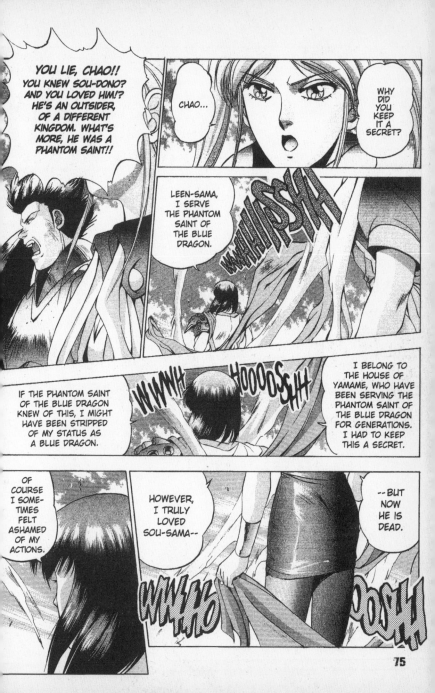

YOU LIE, CHAO!! YOU KNEW SOU-DONO? AND YOU LOVED HIM!? HE'S AN OUTSIDER, OF A DIFFERENT KINGDOM. WHAT'S MORE, HE WAS A PHANTOM SAINT!!

CHAO...

WHY DID YOU KEEP IT A SECRET?

LEEN-SAMA, I SERVE THE PHANTOM SAINT OF THE BLUE DRAGON.

IF THE PHANTOM SAINT OF THE BLUE DRAGON KNEW OF THIS, I MIGHT HAVE BEEN STRIPPED OF MY STATUS AS A BLUE DRAGON.

I BELONG TO THE HOUSE OF YAMAME, WHO HAVE BEEN SERVING THE PHANTOM SAINT OF THE BLUE DRAGON FOR GENERATIONS. I HAD TO KEEP THIS A SECRET.

OF COURSE I SOME- TIMES FELT ASHAMED OF MY ACTIONS.

HOWEVER, I TRULY LOVED SOU-SAMA--

--BUT NOW HE IS DEAD.

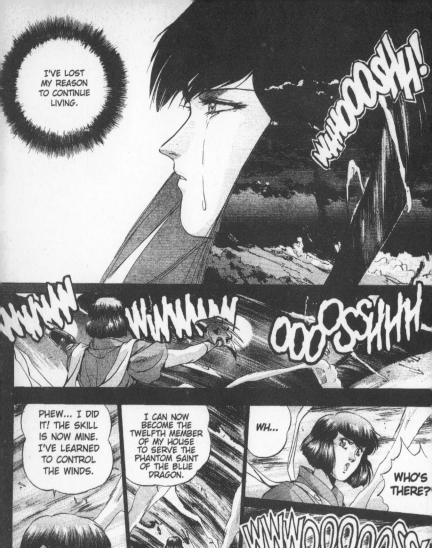

I'VE LOST MY REASON TO CONTINUE LIVING.

WHOOOSSHH!

OOOSSHHH!

PHEW... I DID IT! THE SKILL IS NOW MINE. I'VE LEARNED TO CONTROL THE WINDS.

I CAN NOW BECOME THE TWELFTH MEMBER OF MY HOUSE TO SERVE THE PHANTOM SAINT OF THE BLUE DRAGON.

WH...

WHO'S THERE?

HEY, YOU!

WWWOOOOOSSH

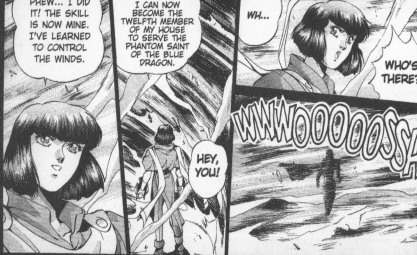

W...WHO IS THIS GUY? HOW COULD HE JUST WALK THROUGH MY TORNADO LIKE THAT?
UHH ...
YOU THERE! WHO ARE YOU?
WHOOOSH
I AM--
I'M SO SORRY. I FORGET MY MANNERS.
I CAN'T SEE MY HAND IN FRONT OF MY FACE IN ALL THIS DUST.
COULD YOU PLEASE TURN DOWN THIS TORNADO A BIT?
FWAP
--SOU, PHANTOM SAINT OF THE RED PHOENIX. I'M ON MY WAY TO SEE THE PHANTOM SAINT OF THE BLUE DRAGON.
WHOO

PHANTOM SAINT... OF THE RED PHOENIX?
SOU...
!!
WHAT? DAMN!!
HUH?!

WWOOOSSHHH
AH...
YOU SHOULD PAY ATTENTION UNTIL YOU'VE FINISHED YOUR SPELL.
SLIP!
Y... YES.
OUCH!!
ARE YOU ALL RIGHT?
Y... YES.
IT SEEMS THAT MY SWORDS-MANSHIP ISN'T PERFECT JUST YET.
HUH? YIKES!
I'LL TAKE YOU TO THE CITY. WHAT'S YOUR NAME?
UM... C... CHAO. MY NAME IS CHAO.
CHAO... THAT'S A CUTE NAME.
WHAT?

FLAP
!!
WHISH!
I'VE GOTTEN A LITTLE TIRED OF WALKING.
I STILL NEED FURTHER TRAINING.
THIS MAN IS...THE PHANTOM SAINT OF THE RED PHOENIX, SOU-SAMA!!

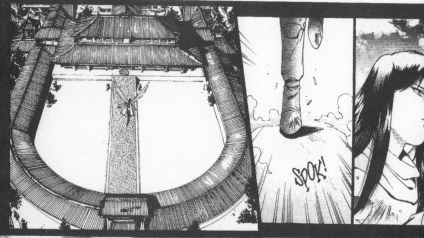

SPOK!

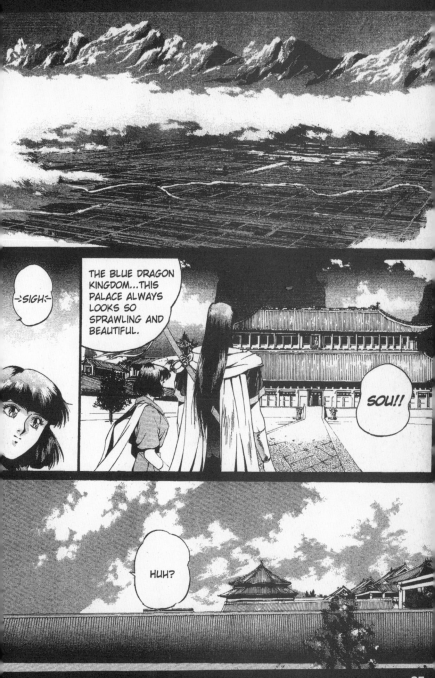

THE BLUE DRAGON KINGDOM...THIS PALACE ALWAYS LOOKS SO SPRAWLING AND BEAUTIFUL.

≥SIGH≤

SOU!!

HUH?

WELCOME!!
IT MUST HAVE BEEN A LONG TRIP, ALL THE WAY INTO TOI.
MEI-DONO.
BOW
MEI-SAMA!!
HUH? YOU... YOU'RE CHAO, AREN'T YOU?
WH AR YO HER
BECAUSE I... I'M...
ALLOW ME TO EXPLAIN.
I ASKE HER T BRING M HERE, T THE BL DRAGO KINGDOM
WHAT?

I GOT LOST ON THE WAY. SHE GUIDED ME HERE.
HEH, HEH. I AM DEEPLY ASHAMED OF MYSELF.
S... SOU-SAMA.
HMM... I SEE.
CHAO, YOU'VE DONE WELL.
THANK YOU, SIR...
PLEASE COME INSIDE, SOU-SAMA.
THANK YOU. MEI-DONO, YOU ARE BLESSED TO HAVE SUCH LOYAL FOLLOWERS.
HOWEVER, I WONDER HOW IT WAS YOU GOT LOST? YOU'D ONLY JUST COME HERE RECENTLY.
HA HA. I NEVER REALIZED THAT I HAVE SUCH A POOR SENSE OF DIRECTION.

AAHHH!
SOU-SAMA!

THANK YOU.

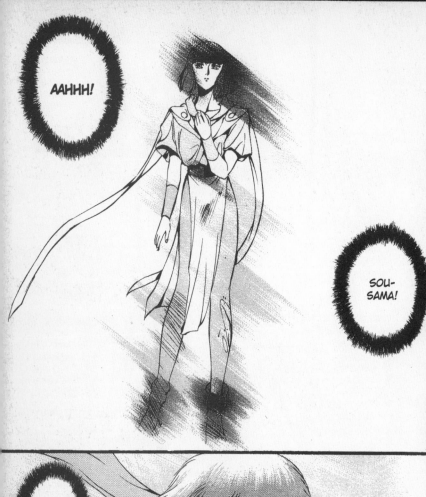

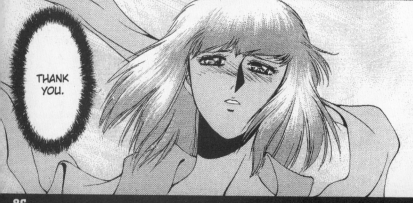

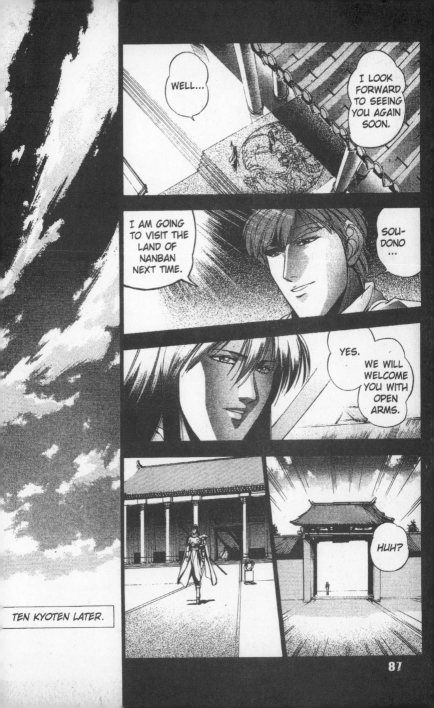

WELL...

I LOOK FORWARD TO SEEING YOU AGAIN SOON.

I AM GOING TO VISIT THE LAND OF NANBAN NEXT TIME.

SOU-DONO...

YES. WE WILL WELCOME YOU WITH OPEN ARMS.

HUH?

TEN KYOTEN LATER.

87

YOU'RE CHAO, RIGHT? WHAT'S WRONG?
SIR...
SSSHHH
MAY I ASK A FAVOR OF YOU?
I WOULD LIKE YOU TO TRAIN ME--
--HARDEN MY SPIRIT, IMPROVE MY SKILLS AND STRENGTHEN MY BODY.
SOU-SAMA...
BUT I AM THE PHANTOM SAINT OF THE RED PHOENIX.
I WILL NOT BE ABLE TO TRAIN YOU AT LENGTH. THIS MUST BE KEPT STRICTLY SECRET.
AS YOU SERVE THE PHANTOM SAINT OF THE BLUE DRAGON--
--YOU WON'T BE ABLE TO TELL PEOPLE ABOUT WHAT YOU ARE TAUGHT BY THOSE OF THE RED PHOENIX!

THAT
DOES
NOT
MATTER!

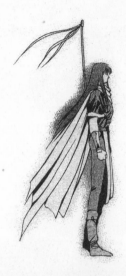

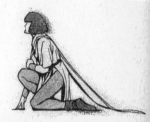

ALL
RIGHT.

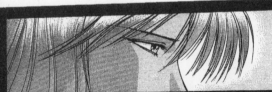

THANK
YOU,
SOU-
SAMA.

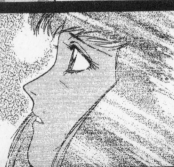

HOWEVER,
SOU-SAMA
WAS IN THE
SAME SITUATION.
IF PEOPLE KNEW
THAT HE HAD
TAUGHT ONE
OF THE BLUE
DRAGON--

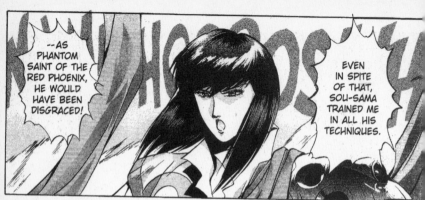

--AS PHANTOM SAINT OF THE RED PHOENIX, HE WOULD HAVE BEEN DISGRACED!

EVEN IN SPITE OF THAT, SOU-SAMA TRAINED ME IN ALL HIS TECHNIQUES.

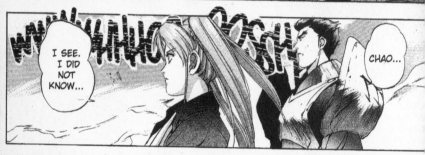

I SEE. I DID NOT KNOW...

CHAO...

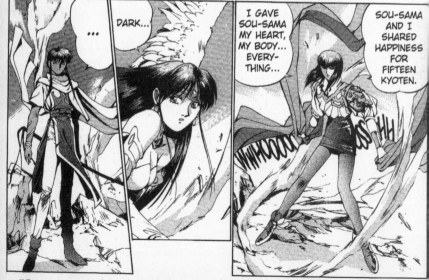

...

DARK...

I GAVE SOU-SAMA MY HEART, MY BODY... EVERYTHING...

SOU-SAMA AND I SHARED HAPPINESS FOR FIFTEEN KYOTEN.

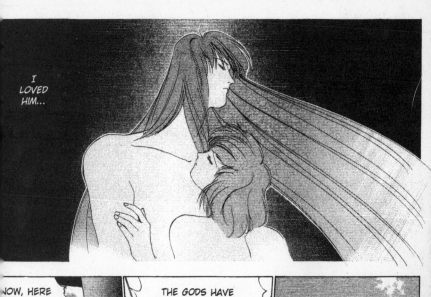

I LOVED HIM...

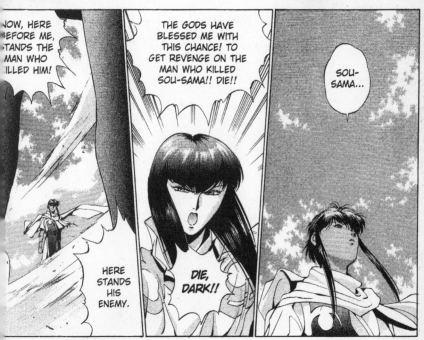

NOW, HERE BEFORE ME, STANDS THE MAN WHO KILLED HIM!

HERE STANDS HIS ENEMY.

THE GODS HAVE BLESSED ME WITH THIS CHANCE! TO GET REVENGE ON THE MAN WHO KILLED SOU-SAMA!! DIE!!

DIE, DARK!!

SOU-SAMA...

WHIRLING WINDS FORM BLADES OF MIGHT!!
GRIP!

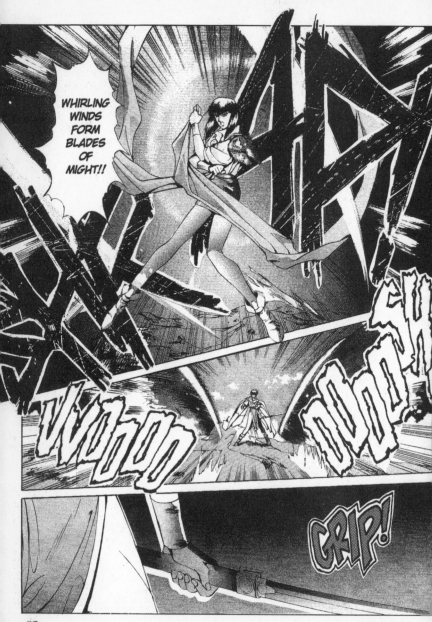

HMM...
NNNOOOOO!!!
DARK!!
THUD!
HEH!
AAAARRGGHHH!

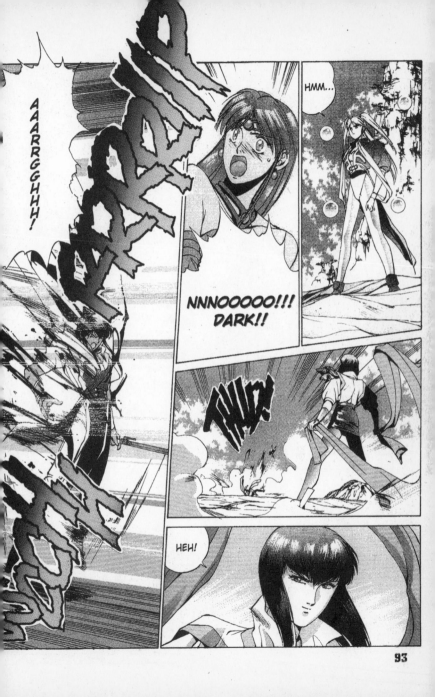

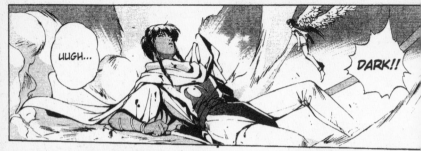

UUGH...

DARK!!

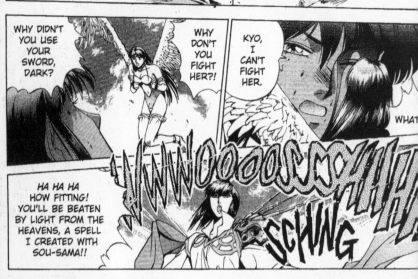

WHY DIDN'T YOU USE YOUR SWORD, DARK?

WHY DON'T YOU FIGHT HER?!

KYO, I CAN'T FIGHT HER.

WHAT

HA HA HA HOW FITTING! YOU'LL BE BEATEN BY LIGHT FROM THE HEAVENS, A SPELL I CREATED WITH SOU-SAMA!!

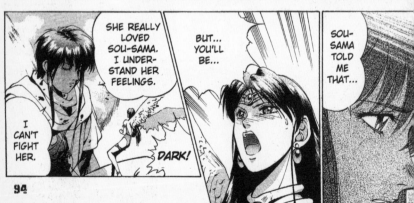

SHE REALLY LOVED SOU-SAMA. I UNDERSTAND HER FEELINGS.

I CAN'T FIGHT HER.

DARK!

BUT... YOU'LL BE...

SOU-SAMA TOLD ME THAT...

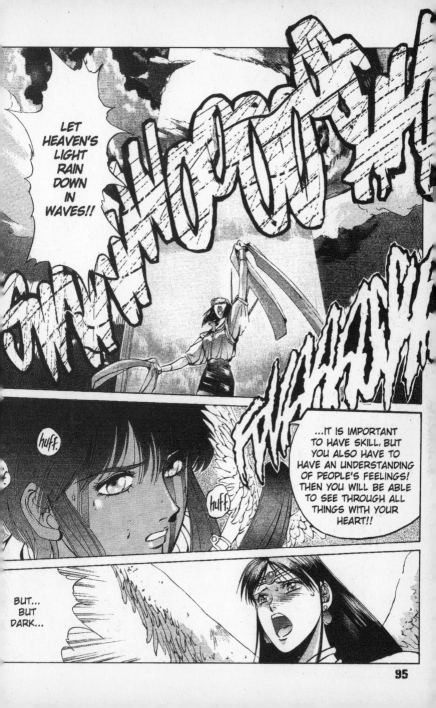

LET HEAVEN'S LIGHT RAIN DOWN IN WAVES!!

huff.

huff.

...IT IS IMPORTANT TO HAVE SKILL, BUT YOU ALSO HAVE TO HAVE AN UNDERSTANDING OF PEOPLE'S FEELINGS! THEN YOU WILL BE ABLE TO SEE THROUGH ALL THINGS WITH YOUR HEART!!

BUT... BUT DARK...

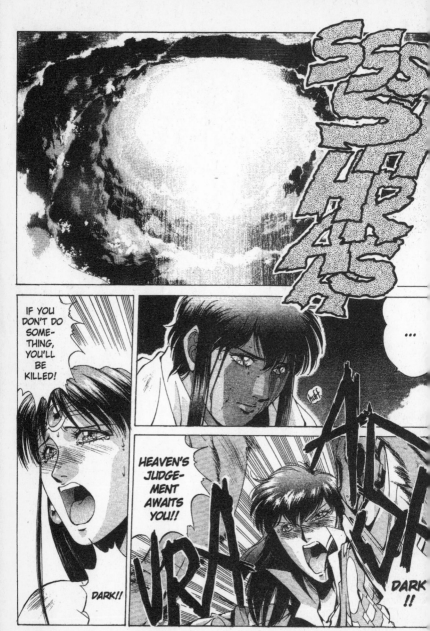

IF YOU DON'T DO SOMETHING, YOU'LL BE KILLED!

HEAVEN'S JUDGEMENT AWAITS YOU!!

huff...

DARK!!

DARK!!

UGHH!!
AAAIIEEEE!
KYO!!

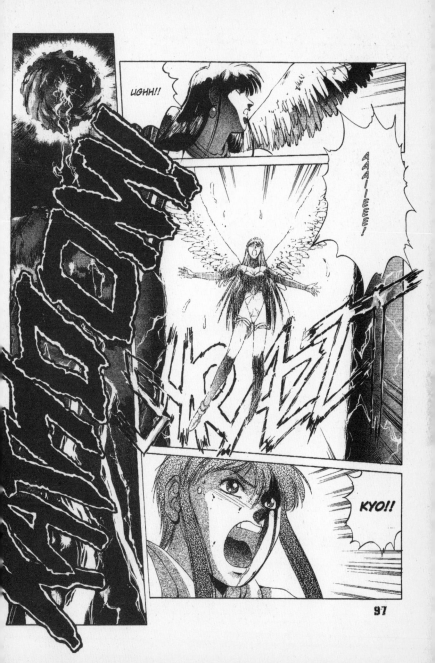

CRAAAAAK!
SOU-SAMA, I DID IT. SOU-SAMA...
UMM
LEEN-SAMA...
SIGH.
WHOOOOOOSH

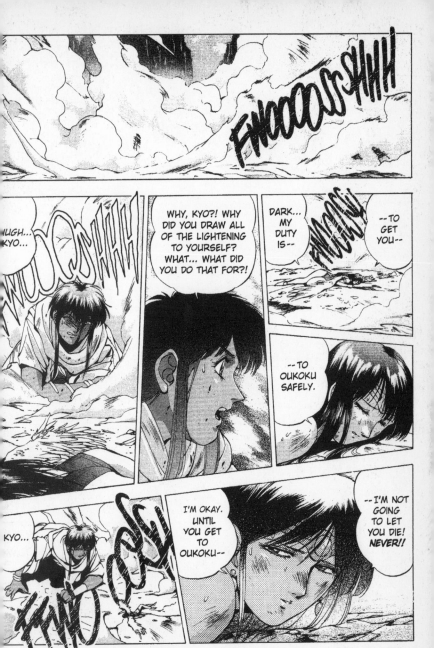

FWOOOSSSHHHH

UGH...
KYO...

WHY, KYO?! WHY DID YOU DRAW ALL OF THE LIGHTENING TO YOURSELF? WHAT... WHAT DID YOU DO THAT FOR?!

DARK... MY DUTY IS--

--TO GET YOU--

--TO OUKOKU SAFELY.

KYO...

I'M OKAY. UNTIL YOU GET TO OUKOKU--

--I'M NOT GOING TO LET YOU DIE! NEVER!!

I WAS CHARGED WITH THE DUTY OF TAKING THE PHANTOM SAINT OF THE RED PHOENIX TO OUKOKU.
BECAUSE... I WAS THE CHOSEN ONE... OUT OF ALL THE SPIRITS...
KYO...
BUT...
AHH...
THUMP
KYO!!

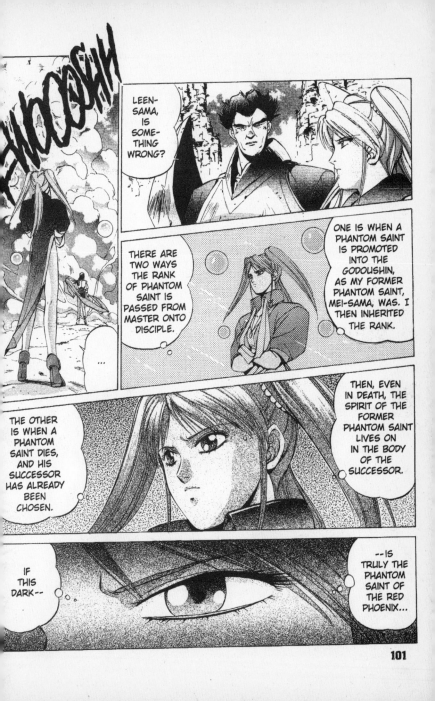

FWOOOOSH

LEEN-SAMA, IS SOMETHING WRONG?

THERE ARE TWO WAYS THE RANK OF PHANTOM SAINT IS PASSED FROM MASTER ONTO DISCIPLE.

ONE IS WHEN A PHANTOM SAINT IS PROMOTED INTO THE GODOUSHIN, AS MY FORMER PHANTOM SAINT, MEI-SAMA, WAS. I THEN INHERITED THE RANK.

...

THE OTHER IS WHEN A PHANTOM SAINT DIES, AND HIS SUCCESSOR HAS ALREADY BEEN CHOSEN.

THEN, EVEN IN DEATH, THE SPIRIT OF THE FORMER PHANTOM SAINT LIVES ON IN THE BODY OF THE SUCCESSOR.

IF THIS DARK--

--IS TRULY THE PHANTOM SAINT OF THE RED PHOENIX...

WHIRLING WINDS FORM BLADES OF MIGHT!!
THAT MEANS ...
NO! IT'S NOT POSSIBLE!! HE'S STILL ALIVE?!?!

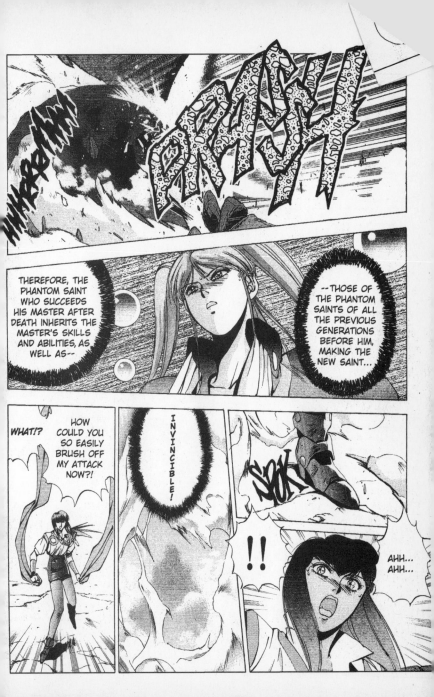

THEREFORE, THE PHANTOM SAINT WHO SUCCEEDS HIS MASTER AFTER DEATH INHERITS THE MASTER'S SKILLS AND ABILITIES, AS WELL AS--

--THOSE OF THE PHANTOM SAINTS OF ALL THE PREVIOUS GENERATIONS BEFORE HIM, MAKING THE NEW SAINT...

WHAT!? HOW COULD YOU SO EASILY BRUSH OFF MY ATTACK NOW?!

INVINCIBLE!

!!

AHH... AHH...

SOU-SAMA ?!?!
IT CAN'T BE !!

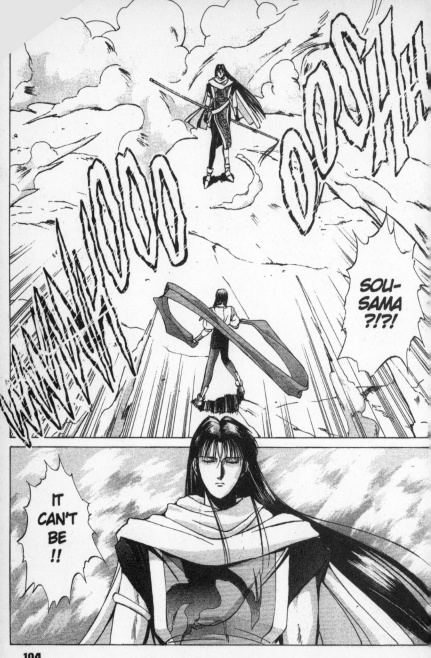

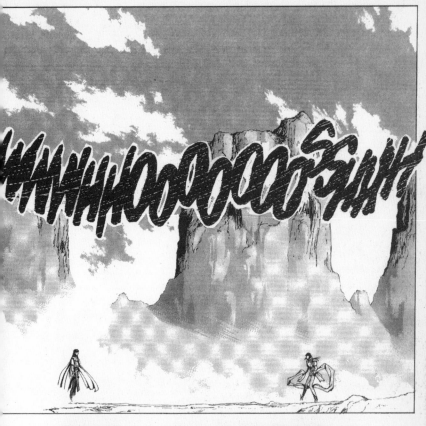

WHAT IS GOING ON?

SOU-SAMA...

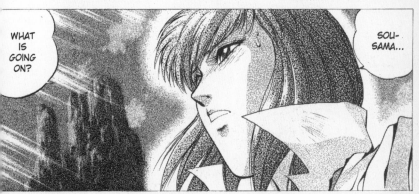

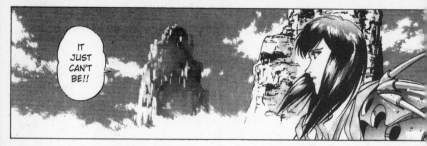

IT JUST CAN'T BE!!

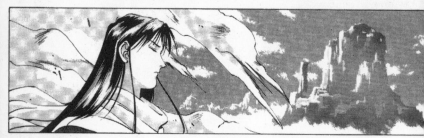

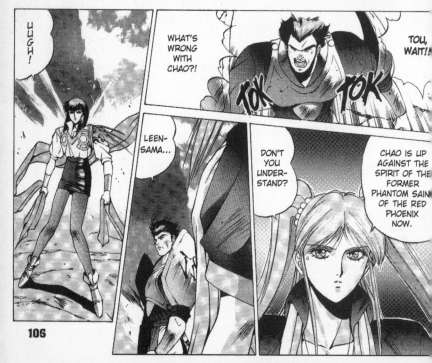

UUGH!

WHAT'S WRONG WITH CHAO?!

TOU, WAIT!!

TOK TOK

LEEN-SAMA...

DON'T YOU UNDER-STAND?

CHAO IS UP AGAINST THE SPIRIT OF THE FORMER PHANTOM SAIN OF THE RED PHOENIX NOW.

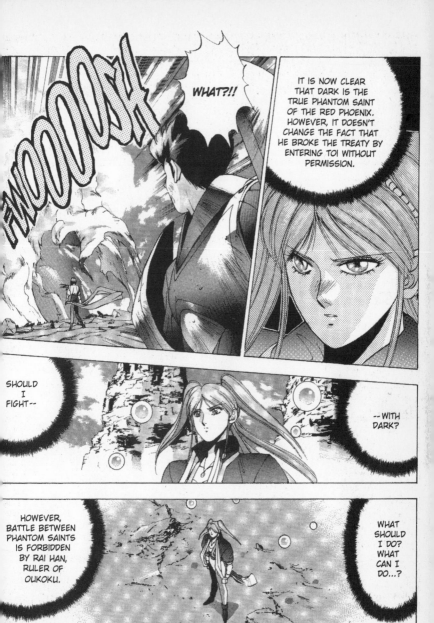

FWOOOOSH

WHAT?!!

IT IS NOW CLEAR THAT DARK IS THE TRUE PHANTOM SAINT OF THE RED PHOENIX. HOWEVER, IT DOESN'T CHANGE THE FACT THAT HE BROKE THE TREATY BY ENTERING TOI WITHOUT PERMISSION.

SHOULD I FIGHT--

-- WITH DARK?

HOWEVER, BATTLE BETWEEN PHANTOM SAINTS IS FORBIDDEN BY RAI HAN, RULER OF OUKOKU.

WHAT SHOULD I DO? WHAT CAN I DO...?

DARK!!
I WON'T FORGIVE YOU!! NEVER!! I WILL NEVER FORGIVE YOU!!
VWOOOSH
ARRGH...
COME OUT! SHOW YOURSELF, DARK!!
USING MAGIC TO SHIELD YOURSELF BEHIND THE FORM OF MY DEAD LOVE!!

UUGH...
I SEE!!
I KNOW IT'S JUST AN ILLUSION, YOU BASTARD!!
I'M GOING TO KILL YOU WITH THE STRONGEST SECRETS OF MY FAMILY!!
AWAA
ASHH
COME OUT, GOD OF WIND!!
SECRET SPELL...
DRAGON...
LIFE...

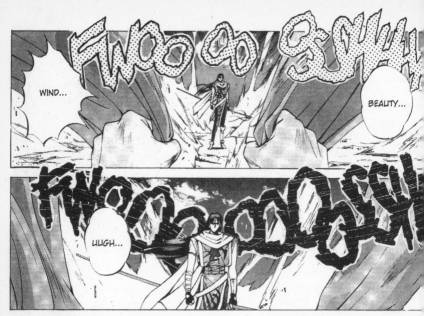

WIND...

BEAUTY...

UUGH...

UUGH...

UMM...

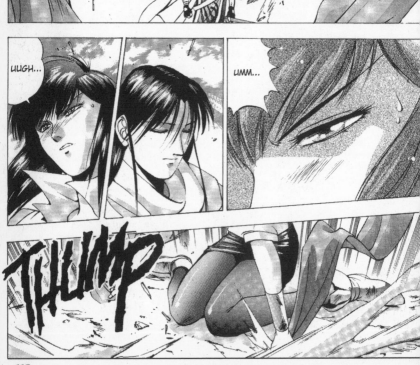

THUMP

110

YOU IDIOT, CHAO!!
STOPPING IN THE MIDDLE OF YOUR SPELL MEANS--
I CAN'T HARM SOU-SAMA...
I JUST CAN'T.
I CAN'T...
FWOOOOM
EVEN THOUGH IT'S JUST AN ILLUSION...
--THE WIND GOD YOU SUMMONED WILL BE RAMPANT!!
FWHOOOOSHH
CHAO, DON'T YOU KNOW THAT?!! COMPLETE THE SPELL!!
SHRAK!
RACK!

THE SECRET SPELLS SUMMON THE GUARDIAN SPIRITS, BUT--
--IF YOU STOP IN THE MIDDLE OF THE SUMMONS, THE SPIRIT WILL--
--TURN ITS FANGS ON YOU!!
WHY, CHAO?!!
AAH!!

LEEN-SAMA!! WE SHOULD LEAVE HERE NOW!! THE WIND GOD'S ANGER IS TOO INTENSE!!
NO, YOU FOOL! WE CAN'T LEAVE CHAO!!
PHOOOSH

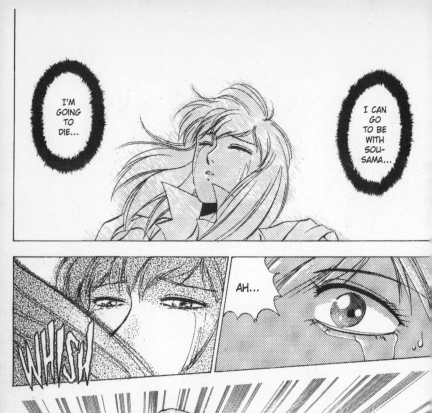

I'M GOING TO DIE...

I CAN GO TO BE WITH SOLI-SAMA...

AH...

WHISH

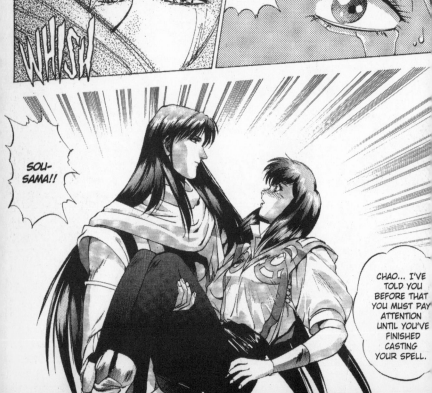

SOLI-SAMA!!

CHAO... I'VE TOLD YOU BEFORE THAT YOU MUST PAY ATTENTION UNTIL YOU'VE FINISHED CASTING YOUR SPELL.

OOOHH...
SOU-SAMA..
LET ME TALK WITH THE WIND GOD.
I WON'T LET YOU DIE, CHAO.
YOU HAVE THINGS TO DO HERE.
YOU'VE BECOME SO BEAUTIFUL, CHAO.
FW WOOOOSHA

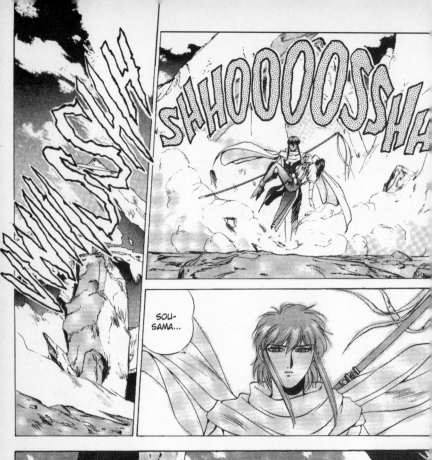

SHHOOOOOSSHH

SHHOOOOSSHH

SOU-
SAMA...

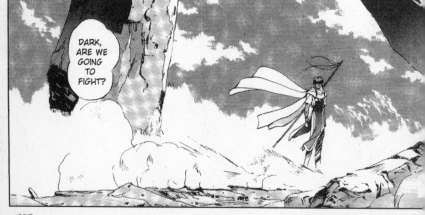

DARK,
ARE WE
GOING
TO
FIGHT?

CHAO!
TAKE HER.
SSSSSHHH
DON'T WORRY. SHE'S ONLY UNCONSCIOUS.
HMPH!
I OWE YOU...
DARK.
...
KYO... IS DEAD. I... I... WHAT SHOULD I DO?
SSSS
SSHHH
IT SEEMS WE HAVE NO CHOICE.
FWOOOSH

I AM READY.
...
BOTH OF YOU, STOP WHERE YOU ARE!!

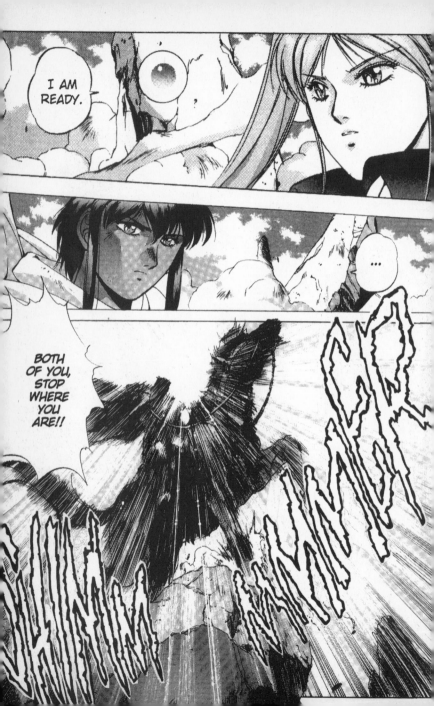

!
WHO IS THAT?
!!

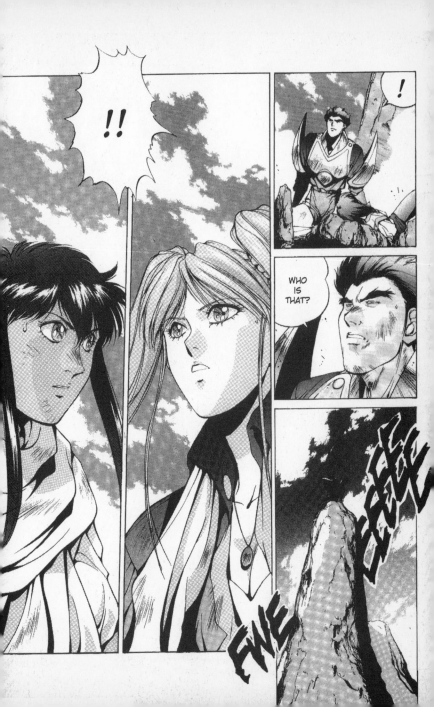

FWHOOOOOOSHH
!?
THAT MUST BE...

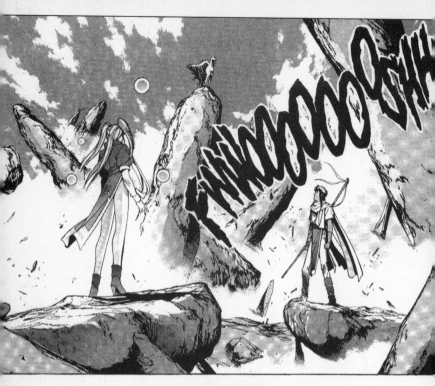

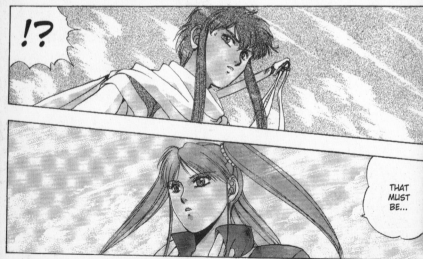

STMP
STMP
TMP
chop!

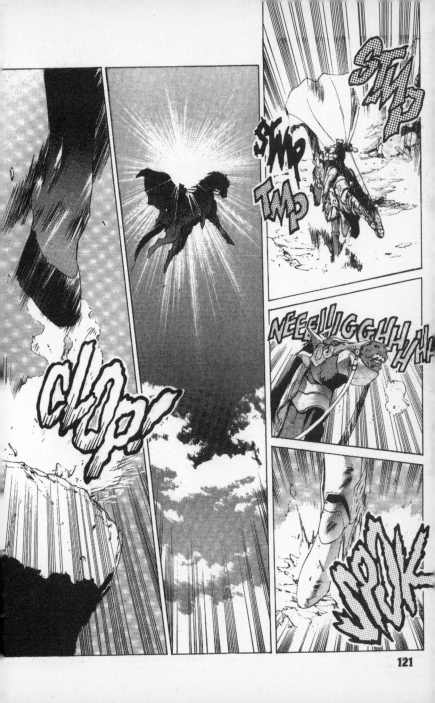

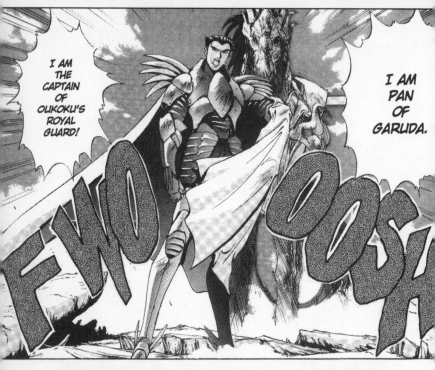

I AM THE CAPTAIN OF OUKOKU'S ROYAL GUARD!

I AM PAN OF GARUDA.

FWO OOSH

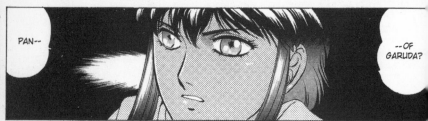

PAN--

--OF GARUDA?

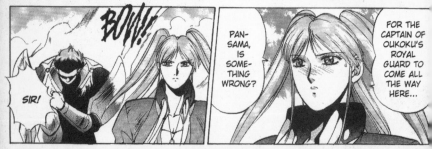

BOW!!

SIR!

PAN-SAMA, IS SOMETHING WRONG?

FOR THE CAPTAIN OF OUKOKU'S ROYAL GUARD TO COME ALL THE WAY HERE...

I CAME HERE TO GREET THE NEW PHANTOM SAINT OF THE RED PHOENIX, DARK-DONO, AS HIS ARRIVAL SEEMED TO HAVE BEEN DELAYED.
HOW-EVER--
--IT SEEMS THERE HAS BEEN A BIT OF TROUBLE HERE.
WHERE IS KYO? I DON'T SEE HER.
KYO IS--
--DEAD.
WHAT!? WHAT HAS HAPPENED, DARK-DONO!!
SHE WAS TRYING TO PROTECT ME...
I NEED BOTH OF YOU TO EXPLAIN EVERYTHING TO ME.

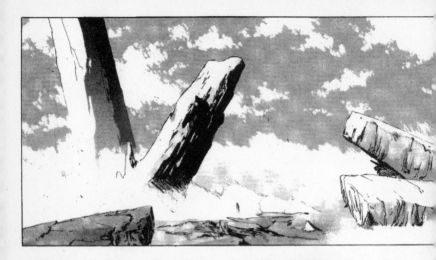

 HMM... I SEE. DARK-DONO WAS AT FAULT FOR ENTERING INTO THE LAND OF TOI WITHOUT PERMISSION.

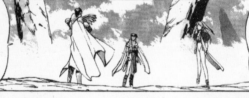 HOWEVER, LEEN-SAMA CHOSE TO CHALLENGE HIM WITHOUT CONFIRMING HIS IDENTITY OR INTENTIONS.

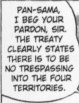 PAN-SAMA, I BEG YOUR PARDON, SIR. THE TREATY CLEARLY STATES THERE IS TO BE NO TRESPASSING INTO THE FOUR TERRITORIES.

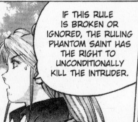 IF THIS RULE IS BROKEN OR IGNORED, THE RULING PHANTOM SAINT HAS THE RIGHT TO UNCONDITIONALLY KILL THE INTRUDER.

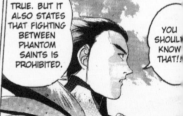 TRUE. BUT IT ALSO STATES THAT FIGHTING BETWEEN PHANTOM SAINTS IS PROHIBITED.

YOU SHOULD KNOW THAT!!

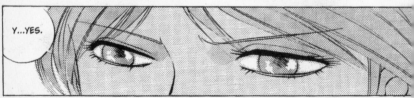 Y...YES.

124

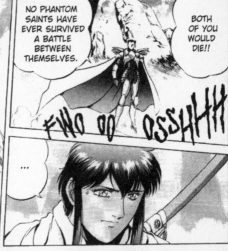

FIGHTING BETWEEN PHANTOM SAINTS ENDANGERS THE TERRITORY AND ITS PEOPLE.

NO PHANTOM SAINTS HAVE EVER SURVIVED A BATTLE BETWEEN THEMSELVES.

BOTH OF YOU WOULD DIE!!

FWOOOOOSSHHH

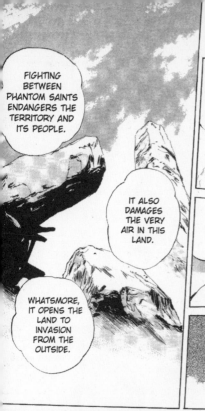

IT ALSO DAMAGES THE VERY AIR IN THIS LAND.

...

WHATSMORE, IT OPENS THE LAND TO INVASION FROM THE OUTSIDE.

...

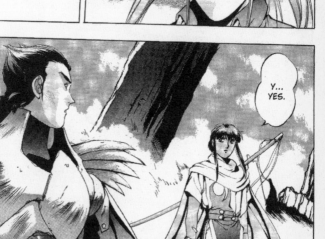

DARK-DONO, DO YOU STILL HAVE KYO'S BODY?

Y... YES.

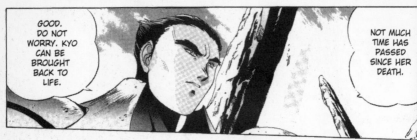

GOOD. DO NOT WORRY. KYO CAN BE BROUGHT BACK TO LIFE.

NOT MUCH TIME HAS PASSED SINCE HER DEATH.

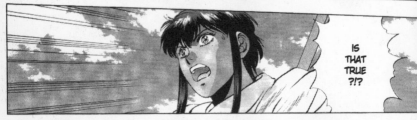

IS THAT TRUE ?!?

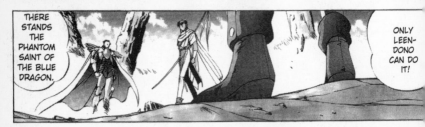

THERE STANDS THE PHANTOM SAINT OF THE BLUE DRAGON.

ONLY LEEN-DONO CAN DO IT!

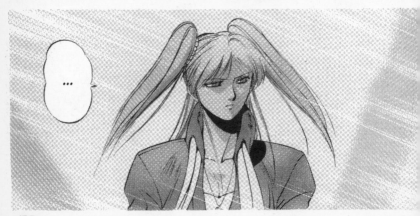

...

CAN YOU...?
LEEN... CAN YOU BRING KYO BACK FROM THE DEAD?
KYO!!
...

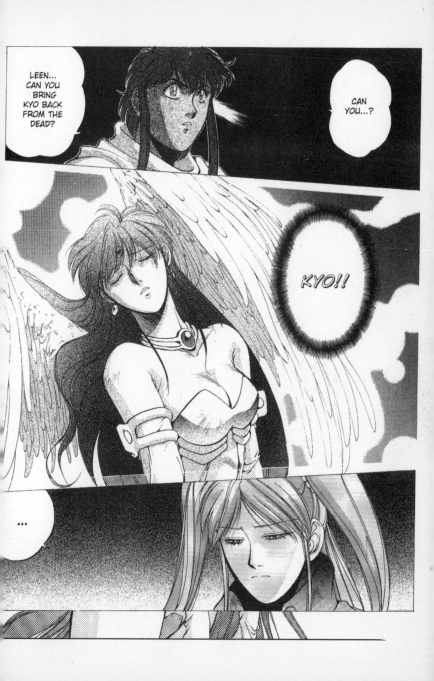

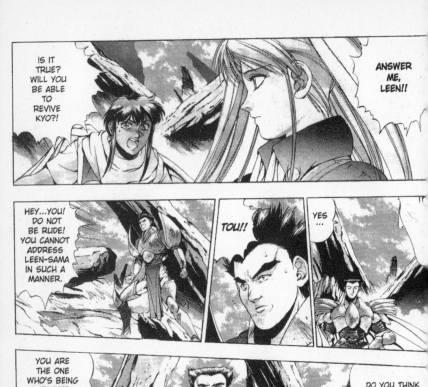

IS IT TRUE? WILL YOU BE ABLE TO REVIVE KYO?!

ANSWER ME, LEEN!!

HEY...YOU! DO NOT BE RUDE! YOU CANNOT ADDRESS LEEN-SAMA IN SUCH A MANNER.

TOU!!

YES...

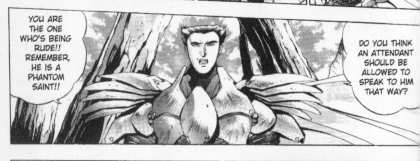

YOU ARE THE ONE WHO'S BEING RUDE!! REMEMBER, HE IS A PHANTOM SAINT!!

DO YOU THINK AN ATTENDANT SHOULD BE ALLOWED TO SPEAK TO HIM THAT WAY?

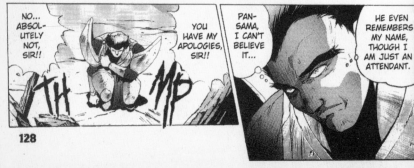

NO...ABSOLUTELY NOT, SIR!!

YOU HAVE MY APOLOGIES, SIR!!

PAN-SAMA, I CAN'T BELIEVE IT...

HE EVEN REMEMBERS MY NAME, THOUGH I AM JUST AN ATTENDANT.

TH MP

IN ANY CASE, BOTH PARTIES SHALL BE PUNISHED HERE. FIRST, LEEN-SAMA...
...
I WOULD LIKE YOU TO BRING KYO BACK TO LIFE.
I UNDERSTAND, SIR. I WILL DO AS YOU ASK.
GRAB

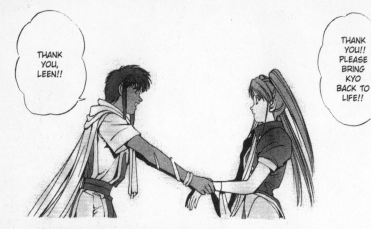

THANK YOU, LEEN!!

THANK YOU!! PLEASE BRING KYO BACK TO LIFE!!

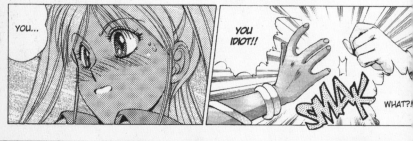

YOU...

YOU IDIOT!!

SMAK

WHAT?!

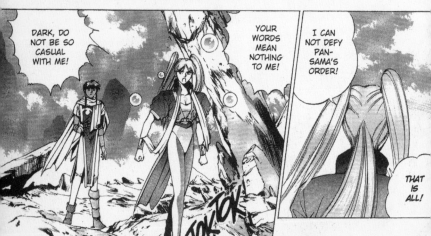

DARK, DO NOT BE SO CASUAL WITH ME!

YOUR WORDS MEAN NOTHING TO ME!

I CAN NOT DEFY PAN-SAMA'S ORDER!

THAT IS ALL!

TOK TOK

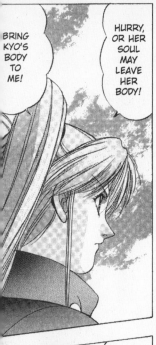

BRING KYO'S BODY TO ME!

HURRY, OR HER SOUL MAY LEAVE HER BODY!

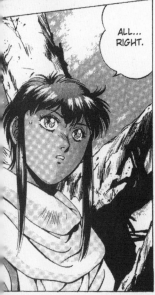

ALL... RIGHT.

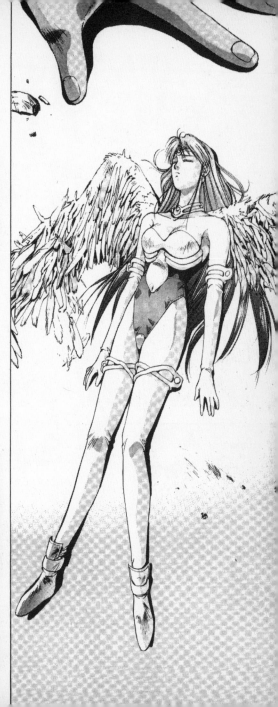

KYO...
HMPH!
...
THANK YOU.
ZZZT KRSHMMM

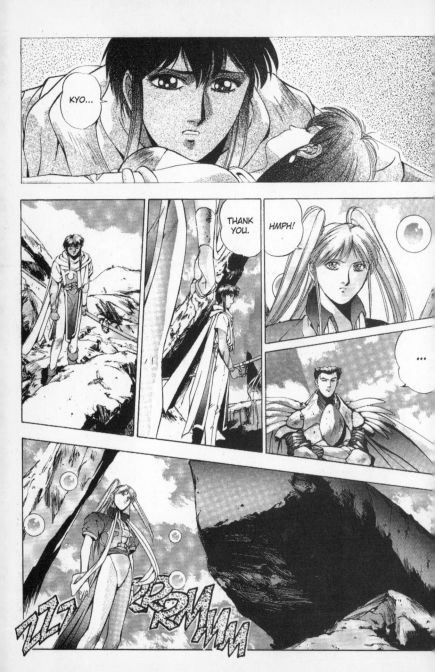

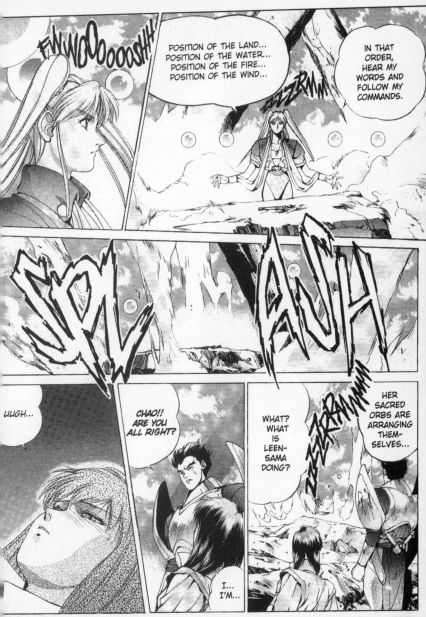

FWWNOOOOOOSHH!

POSITION OF THE LAND...
POSITION OF THE WATER...
POSITION OF THE FIRE...
POSITION OF THE WIND...

IN THAT ORDER, HEAR MY WORDS AND FOLLOW MY COMMANDS.

ZZZZRMM

SPZ

BASH

UUGH...

CHAO!! ARE YOU ALL RIGHT?

WHAT? WHAT IS LEEN-SAMA DOING?

ZZZZZRMMMM

HER SACRED ORBS ARE ARRANGING THEM- SELVES...

I... I'M...

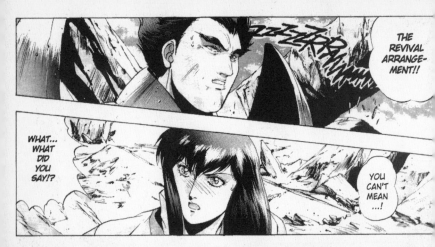

THE REVIVAL ARRANGEMENT!!

WHAT... WHAT DID YOU SAY!?

YOU CAN'T MEAN...!

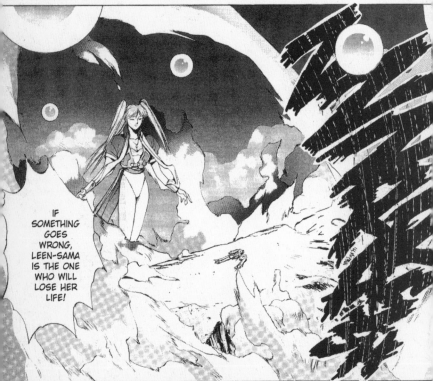

IF SOMETHING GOES WRONG, LEEN-SAMA IS THE ONE WHO WILL LOSE HER LIFE!

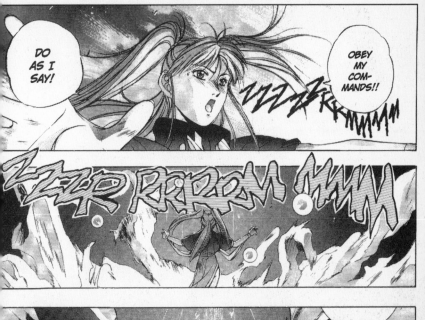

DO AS I SAY!

OBEY MY COM-MANDS!!

ZZZZRKMMMM

ZZZR RRRM MUM

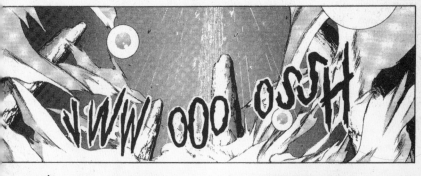

VWW OOO OSSH

HSSO

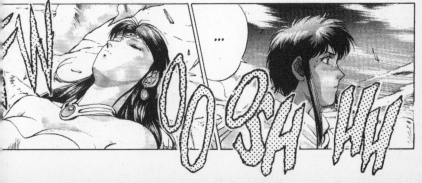

W

OO SH HY

...

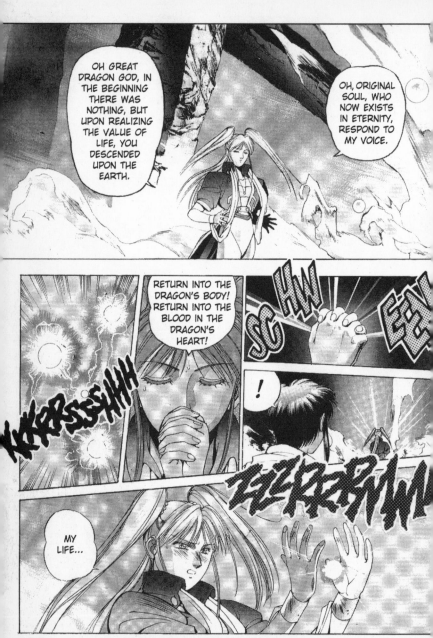

OH GREAT DRAGON GOD, IN THE BEGINNING THERE WAS NOTHING, BUT UPON REALIZING THE VALUE OF LIFE, YOU DESCENDED UPON THE EARTH.

OH, ORIGINAL SOUL, WHO NOW EXISTS IN ETERNITY, RESPOND TO MY VOICE.

RETURN INTO THE DRAGON'S BODY! RETURN INTO THE BLOOD IN THE DRAGON'S HEART!

!

MY LIFE...

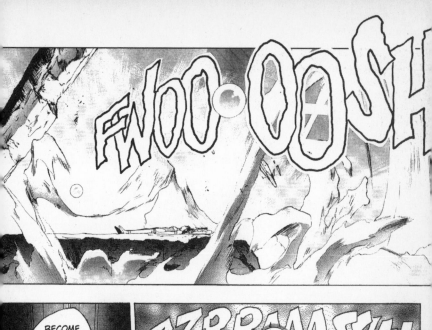

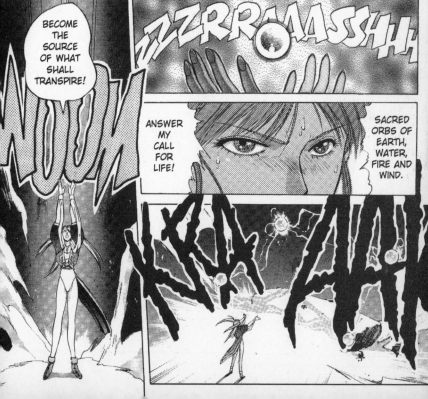

BECOME THE SOURCE OF WHAT SHALL TRANSPIRE!

ANSWER MY CALL FOR LIFE!

SACRED ORBS OF EARTH, WATER, FIRE AND WIND.

SCHRZZAP
SCHRZZAP
SSHOO
HMRRMMM
BWOOOMM

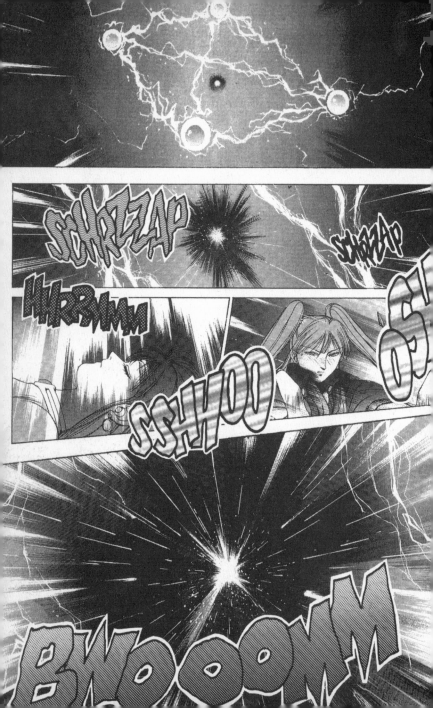

W... WHAT'S THAT? THAT BLACK ABYSS?
IT'S THE BEGINNING OF EVERYTHING.
WHOOOSH
!
THE BEGIN- NING...

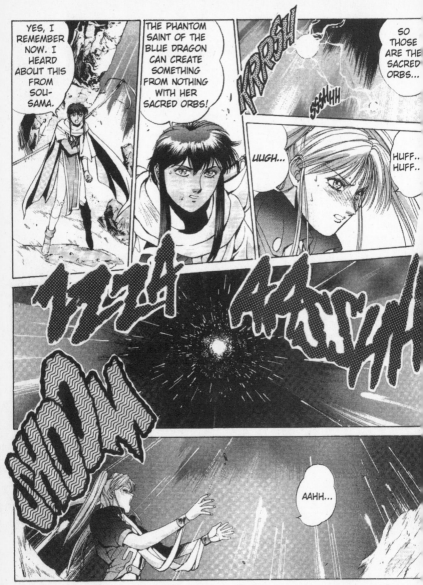

YES, I REMEMBER NOW. I HEARD ABOUT THIS FROM SOU-SAMA.

THE PHANTOM SAINT OF THE BLUE DRAGON CAN CREATE SOMETHING FROM NOTHING WITH HER SACRED ORBS!

SO THOSE ARE THE SACRED ORBS...

KRRRSH

SSSHHH

UUGH...

HUFF.. HUFF..

AAHH...

YES, BUT THOSE ARE NOT ALL OF LEEN-SAMA'S SACRED ORBS.
!
WHAT DO YOU MEAN?
ORIGINALLY THERE WERE FIVE!!
BUT NOW SHE HAS ONLY FOUR - EARTH, WATER, FIRE AND WIND.
WHOOOSH
HEAR MY VOICE!! GIVE ME THE POWER!!
ON THIS LAND, WHERE I STAND! BEFORE THE BLUE DRAGON!!

AARRGH!!!

LEEN-SAMA!!

...

UUGH...

FWWWWOO
OOOOSH!!
DARK!
LEAP!
KYO!
THIS IS WONDER-FUL!
DARK...
KYO!
PAN-SAMA...

LEEN-DONO, YOU'VE DONE WELL.
TH... THANK YOU.
HUFF...
HUFF...
PUFF...
LEEN-SAMA!
TOK! TOK!
LEEN-SAMA!
COUGH... COUGH...
COUGH
COUGH...
LEEN ...?
THUMP
HUFF...
PUFF...
HUFF...

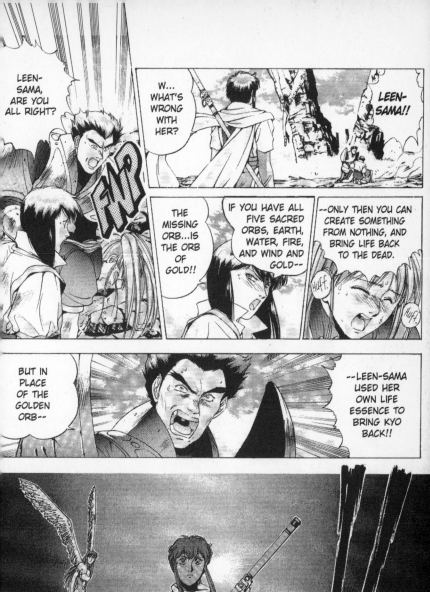

LEEN-SAMA, ARE YOU ALL RIGHT?

W... WHAT'S WRONG WITH HER?

LEEN-SAMA!!

THE MISSING ORB...IS THE ORB OF GOLD!!

IF YOU HAVE ALL FIVE SACRED ORBS, EARTH, WATER, FIRE, AND WIND AND GOLD--

--ONLY THEN YOU CAN CREATE SOMETHING FROM NOTHING, AND BRING LIFE BACK TO THE DEAD.

HUFF.

HUFF.

BUT IN PLACE OF THE GOLDEN ORB--

--LEEN-SAMA USED HER OWN LIFE ESSENCE TO BRING KYO BACK!!

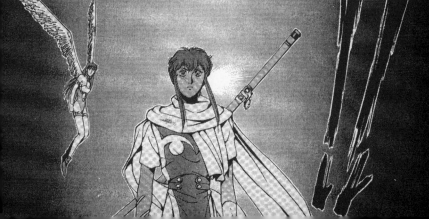

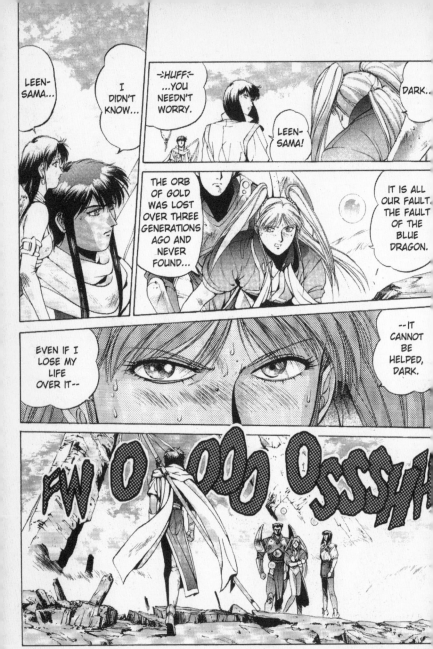

LEEN-SAMA...

I DIDN'T KNOW...

-÷HUFF÷- ...YOU NEEDN'T WORRY.

LEEN-SAMA!

DARK...

THE ORB OF GOLD WAS LOST OVER THREE GENERATIONS AGO AND NEVER FOUND...

IT IS ALL OUR FAULT. THE FAULT OF THE BLUE DRAGON.

EVEN IF I LOSE MY LIFE OVER IT--

--IT CANNOT BE HELPED, DARK.

FW'O OO OSSSH

HEH HEH. FEEL FREE TO FORGET.
I WILL NEVER FORGET THIS.
TH... THANK YOU SO MUCH, LEEN-SAMA...
THANK YOU, LEEN!!
I APPRECIATE IT AS WELL.
HMM...
SLUMP!

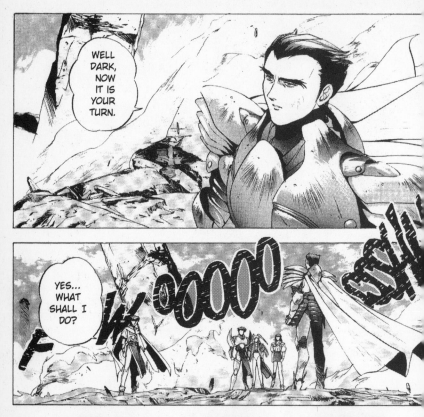

WELL DARK, NOW IT IS YOUR TURN.

YES... WHAT SHALL I DO?

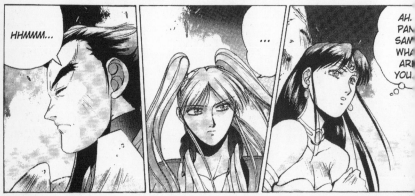

HHMMM...

...

AH. PAN... SAN... WHA... ARE YOU...

I SHALL KEEP THE SWORD OF THE RED PHOENIX, THE PROOF YOU ARE A PHANTOM SAINT.
WHOOSH
DARK-DONO!
WHAT ?!!
NO!! NOT THAT!!

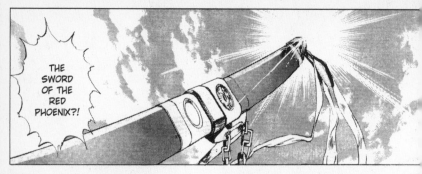

THE SWORD OF THE RED PHOENIX?!

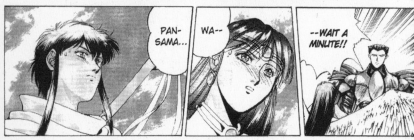

PAN-SAMA...

WA--

--WAIT A MINUTE!!

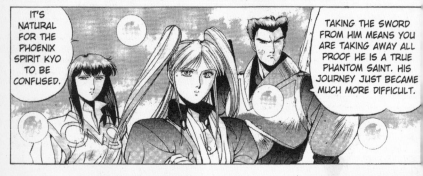

IT'S NATURAL FOR THE PHOENIX SPIRIT KYO TO BE CONFUSED.

TAKING THE SWORD FROM HIM MEANS YOU ARE TAKING AWAY ALL PROOF HE IS A TRUE PHANTOM SAINT. HIS JOURNEY JUST BECAME MUCH MORE DIFFICULT.

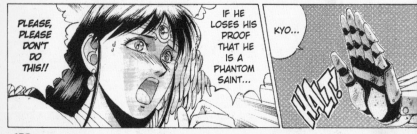

PLEASE, PLEASE DON'T DO THIS!!

IF HE LOSES HIS PROOF THAT HE IS A PHANTOM SAINT...

KYO...

I UNDER-STAND WHAT YOU ARE TRYING TO SAY.
HOWEVER, FROM WHAT I UNDER-STAND--
--I BELIEVE DARK-DONO NEEDS TO LEARN WHAT BEING A PHANTOM SAINT IS ON HIS OWN.
BUT... BUT...
THE SWORD OF THE RED PHOENIX IS PROOF HE IS A PHANTOM SAINT, BUT IT IS ALSO A POWERFUL WEAPON.
IF HE DOESN'T HAVE THE SWORD, HOW WILL HE SURVIVE THE VARIOUS OBSTACLES THAT STAND BEFORE HIM?
ARE YOU SAYING HE WON'T BE ABLE TO SURVIVE?
KYO, IF HE CANNOT OVERCOME CHALLENGES WITHOUT USING A WEAPON--
--HOW CAN HE BE A TRUE PHANTOM SAINT?!
BUT... BUT... BUT...
KYO...

D... DARK...
KYO, IT'S ALL RIGHT.
BUT... BUT... DARK...
I THINK PAN-SAMA IS RIGHT. I AM HONORED TO RELINQUISH THE SWORD OF THE RED PHOENIX TO HIM.
DARK...
PAN-SAMA...
YES.
SWISH!
PLEASE KEEP THIS FOR ME.
I SHALL.

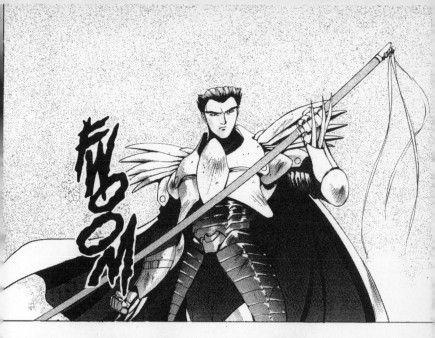

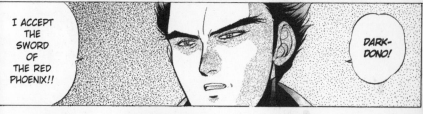

I ACCEPT THE SWORD OF THE RED PHOENIX!!

DARK-DONO!

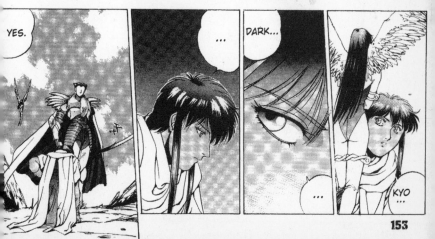

YES.

...

DARK...

...

KYO...

153

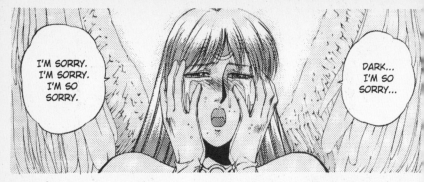

DARK... I'M SO SORRY...
I'M SORRY. I'M SORRY. I'M SO SORRY.
THANK YOU.
DARK.
BUT... BUT...
KYO...
THE TRUTH OF THE MATTER IS, I'M REALLY TO BLAME.
DON'T WORRY, KYO.
HIEN, COME TO ME!!
CLOP! CLOP!

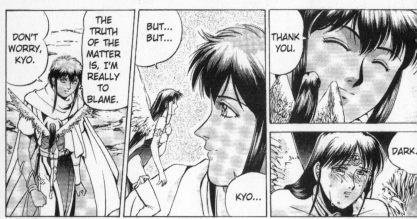

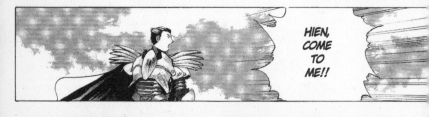

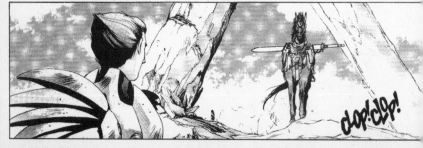

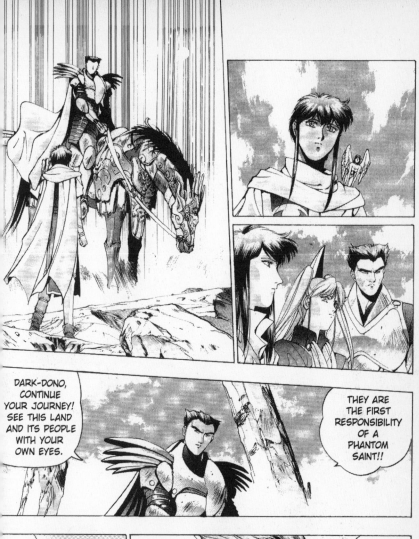

DARK-DONO, CONTINUE YOUR JOURNEY! SEE THIS LAND AND ITS PEOPLE WITH YOUR OWN EYES.

THEY ARE THE FIRST RESPONSIBILITY OF A PHANTOM SAINT!!

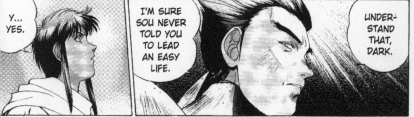

Y... YES.

I'M SURE SOU NEVER TOLD YOU TO LEAD AN EASY LIFE.

UNDERSTAND THAT, DARK.

155

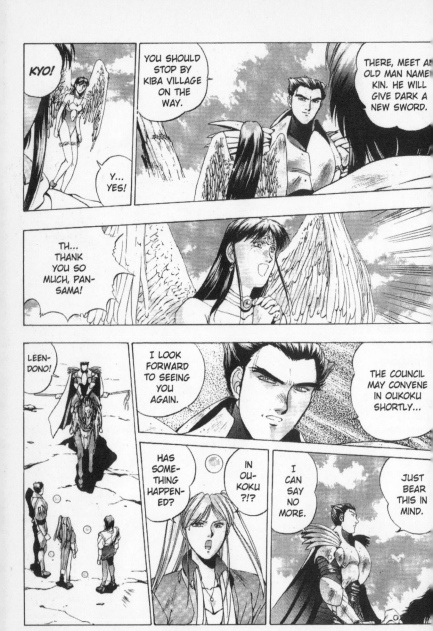

KYO!

YOU SHOULD STOP BY KIBA VILLAGE ON THE WAY.

THERE, MEET AN OLD MAN NAMED KIN. HE WILL GIVE DARK A NEW SWORD.

Y... YES!

TH... THANK YOU SO MUCH, PAN-SAMA!

LEEN-DONO!

I LOOK FORWARD TO SEEING YOU AGAIN.

THE COUNCIL MAY CONVENE IN OUKOKU SHORTLY...

HAS SOME-THING HAPPEN-ED?

IN OU-KOKU?!?

I CAN SAY NO MORE.

JUST BEAR THIS IN MIND.

WELL...
LET'S GO, HIEN!!
GALLOP
YES!
RAI HAN WILL BE AWAITING YOUR ARRIVAL!!
DARK-DONO!! I SHALL SEE YOU IN OUKOKU!!
CLOPCLOP

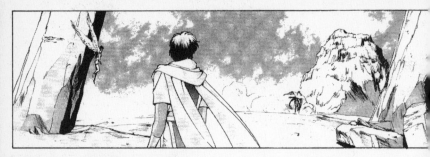

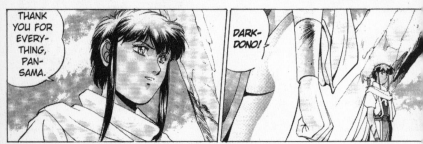

THANK YOU FOR EVERYTHING, PAN-SAMA.

DARK-DONO!

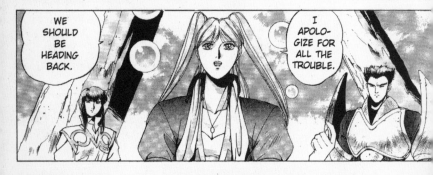

WE SHOULD BE HEADING BACK.

I APOLOGIZE FOR ALL THE TROUBLE.

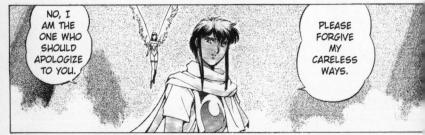

NO, I AM THE ONE WHO SHOULD APOLOGIZE TO YOU.

PLEASE FORGIVE MY CARELESS WAYS.

TAKE CARE, DARK.
WE WILL MEET AGAIN SOMEDAY.
YES, OF COURSE.
FWOOSH

SO, SHALL WE GET GOING, TOO?
YEAH.

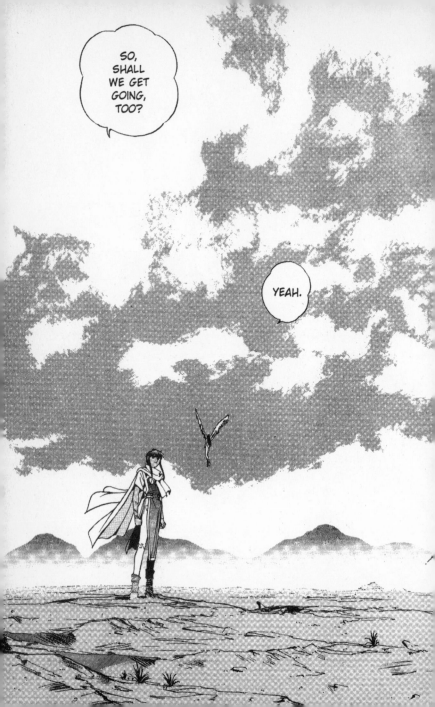

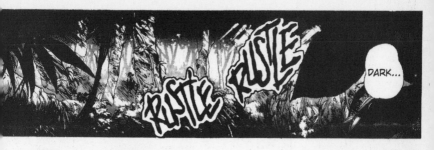
DARK...

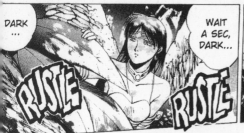
DARK
...

WAIT A SEC, DARK...

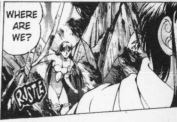
WHERE ARE WE?

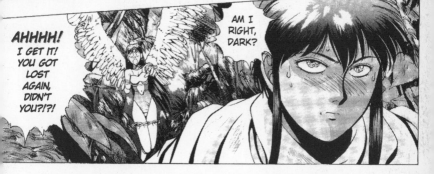
AHHHH! I GET IT! YOU GOT LOST AGAIN, DIDN'T YOU?!?!

AM I RIGHT, DARK?

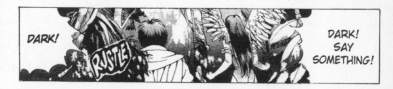
DARK!

DARK! SAY SOMETHING!

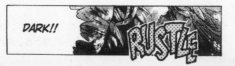
DARK!!

THIS SERIES WAS FIRST PUBLISHED IN *NEW TYPE MAGAZINE* IN JAPAN, AROUND THE SAME TIME THE *SILENT MOBIUS* SERIES BEGAN. THE DRAWINGS HAVE CHANGED A LOT SINCE THEN. I DIDN'T RETOUCH A SINGLE FRAME FOR THIS VERSION. I GET SO EMBARRASSED WHEN I LOOK AT THESE DRAWINGS, MY FACE TURNS BEET RED. ANYWAY, DARK ANGEL STARTED WITH THE ROUGH SKETCHES BELOW. THESE ARE THE ORIGINALS.

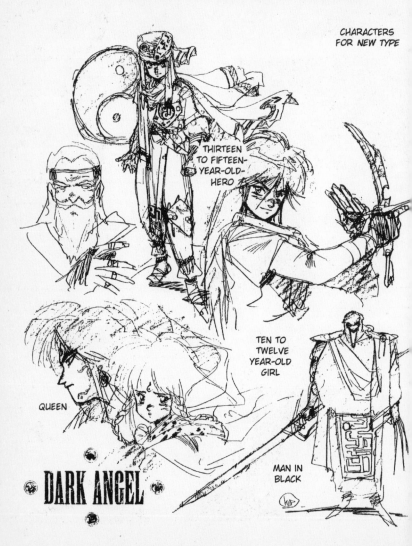

CHARACTERS FOR *NEW TYPE*

THIRTEEN TO FIFTEEN-YEAR-OLD HERO

TEN TO TWELVE YEAR-OLD GIRL

QUEEN

DARK ANGEL

MAN IN BLACK

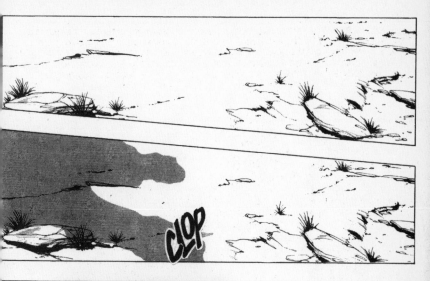

CLOP

WHEW.

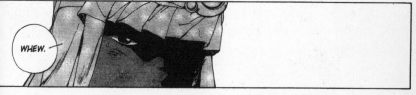

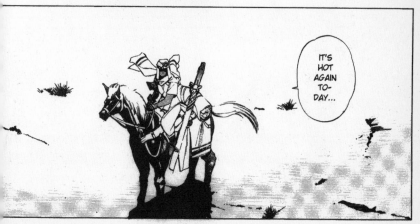

IT'S HOT AGAIN TODAY...

EEEK!
LAP LAP.

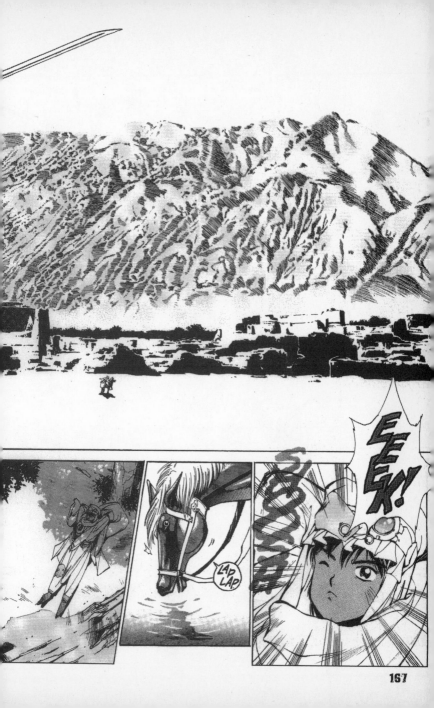

WH...
!!
WHAT?!
HELP!

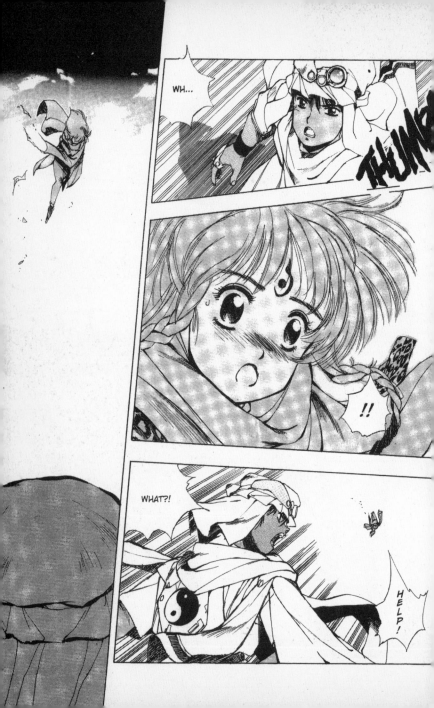

HUFF.
TOK TOK
TOK TOK
THOSE TWO...

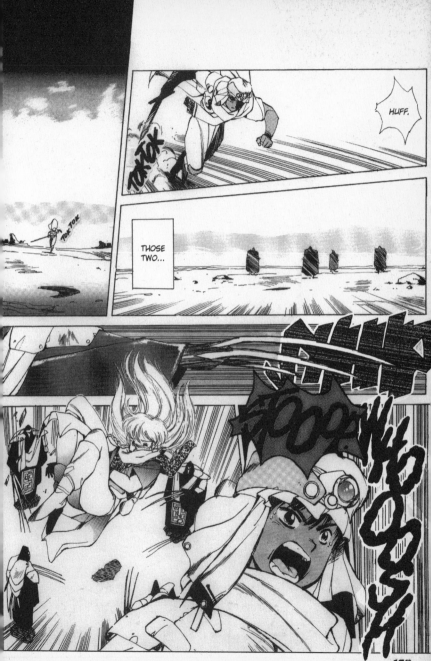

KIYAAH!!
YOU SCUM!
FWISH!

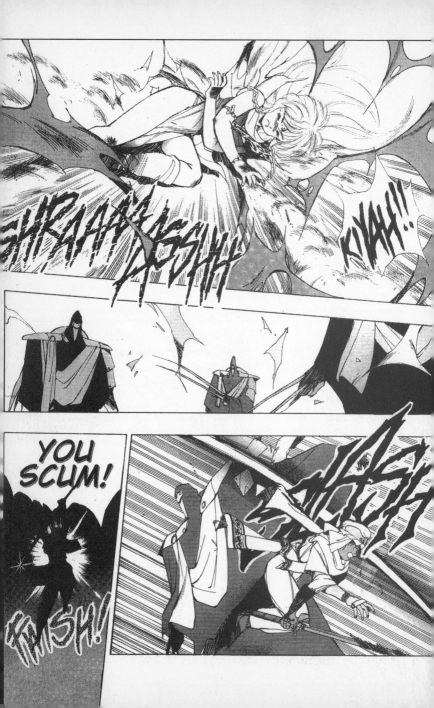

MUD!?
ARRGH!
YANK
UHH...
UGGH!
THUD!

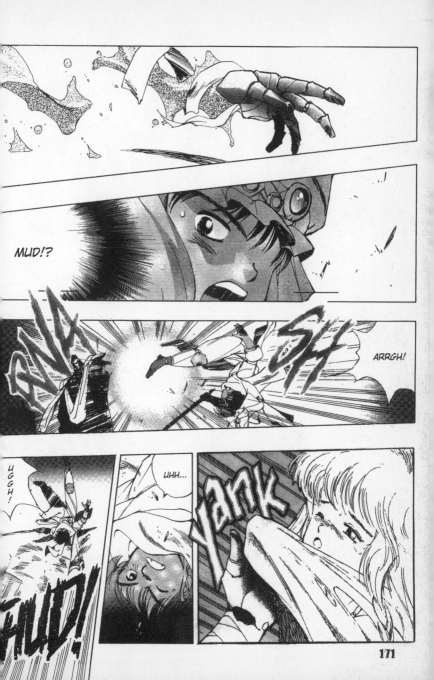

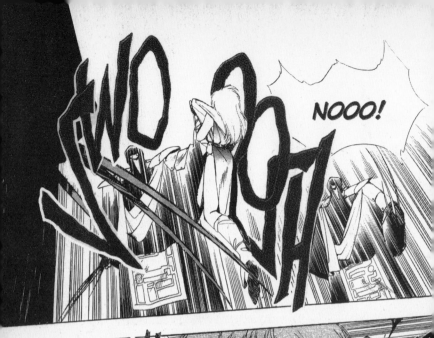

NOOO!

LEAVE HER ALONE!!

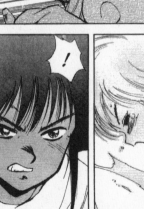

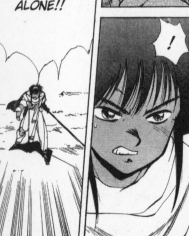

IN THE NAME OF THIS SWORD, I RELEASE THE SEAL...

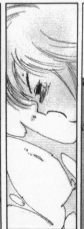

172

VWOOOSHH
!?
FWWISSHH
SWAASH

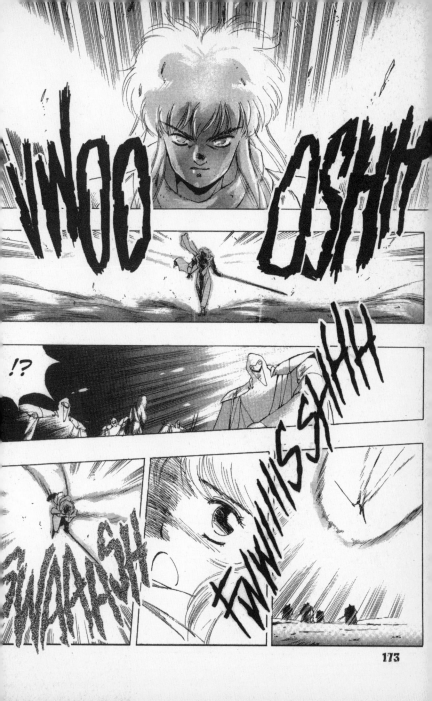

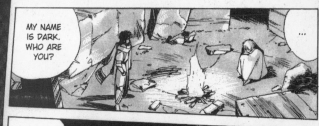

MY NAME IS DARK. WHO ARE YOU?

...

WHY WERE THOSE GUYS CHASING YOU?

...

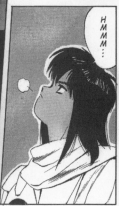

HMMM...

I DON'T KNOW.

!

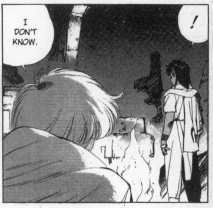

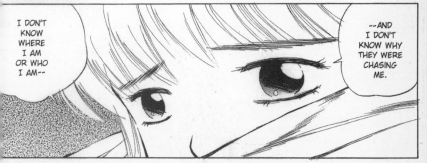

I DON'T KNOW WHERE I AM OR WHO I AM--

--AND I DON'T KNOW WHY THEY WERE CHASING ME.

WHERE DID YOU GET THAT POWER?
WHAT ARE YOU?!
FWOOOSHA
I'VE BEEN LIVING ALONE ON THIS GREAT LAND SINCE I WAS A KID.
CLINK.
THIS POWER WAS GIVEN TO ME TO WATCH OVER THIS LAND FROM BEGINNING TO END.
SHAP.

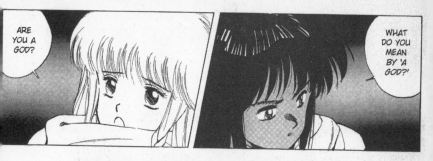

ARE YOU A GOD?

WHAT DO YOU MEAN BY 'A GOD?'

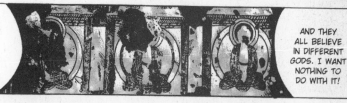

I'VE MET A LOT OF PEOPLE HERE WHO BELIEVE IN GODS.

AND THEY ALL BELIEVE IN DIFFERENT GODS. I WANT NOTHING TO DO WITH IT!

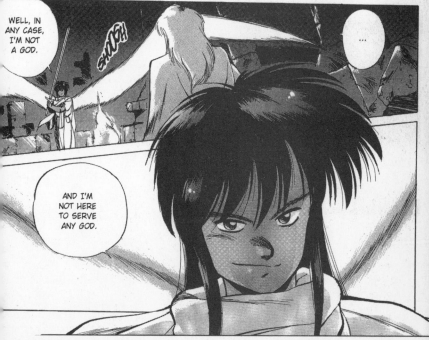

WELL, IN ANY CASE, I'M NOT A GOD.

SHUNK

...

AND I'M NOT HERE TO SERVE ANY GOD.

SOMEONE HAS ENTERED MY SACRED SPACE.
UGH... WHO'S THERE?
WHO IS IT?!
FLASH
MY PURE POWER... MY PURE HEART...
PLOP
THOSE TWO...
HMPH... THE FINAL DAY HAS COME.
WHO IS THAT GIRL?
!!
plop plop
UU...
UGH...

KILL THEM!!

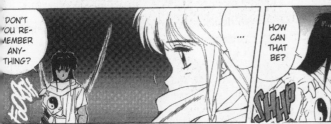

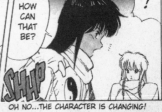

OH NO...THE CHARACTER IS CHANGING!

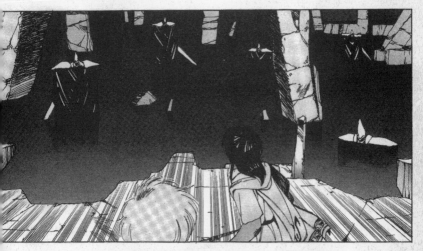

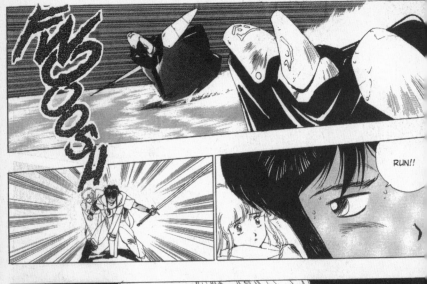

RUN!!

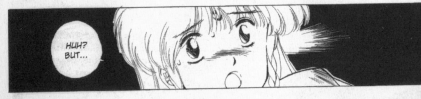

HUH? BUT...

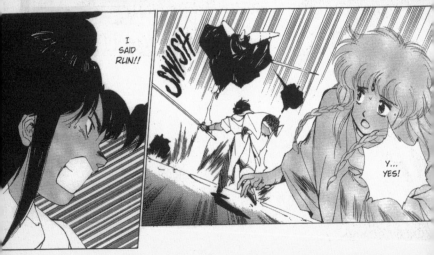

I SAID RUN!!

SWISH

Y.... YES!

DAMN!
NOOO!!
WHAT
HE...!?
AHH!
SLASH
SLICE

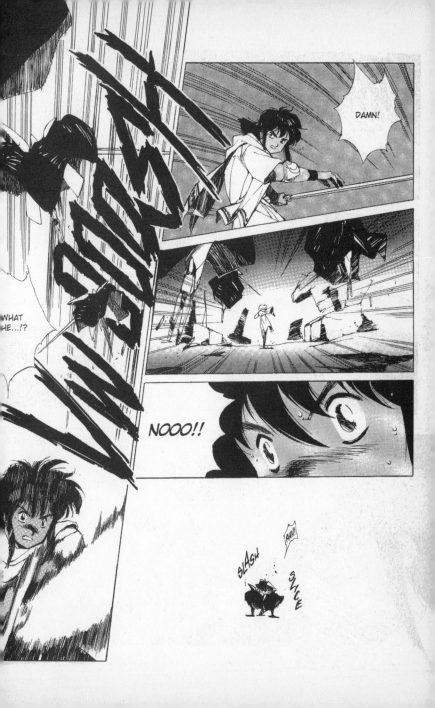

AHH...
SWOOSH
I...
I...

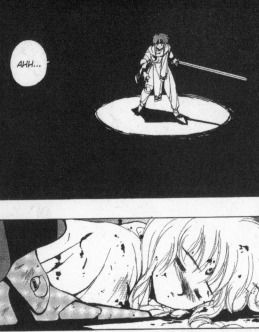

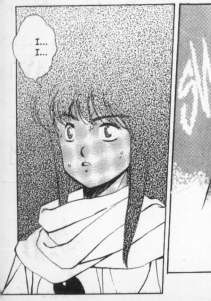

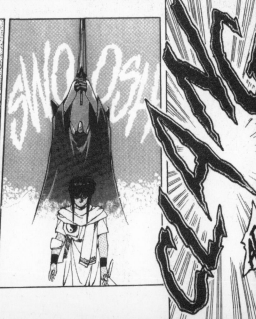

HIYAH!
NOT A MUD DOLL THIS TIME!
SPLASH
SWHOOSH
HEY, WAIT!
plash

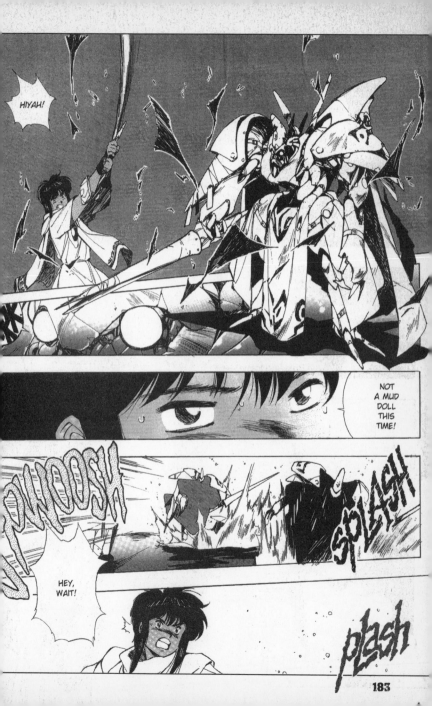

KAPLOOOSH
BLOOP
YOU HAVE DEFILED MY SACRED SPACE... WHO ARE YOU?!
!!
DAMN!
SSSSHHHH

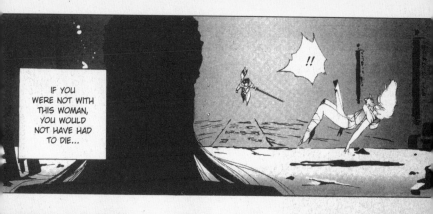

IF YOU WERE NOT WITH THIS WOMAN, YOU WOULD NOT HAVE HAD TO DIE...

!!

KILL HIM!!

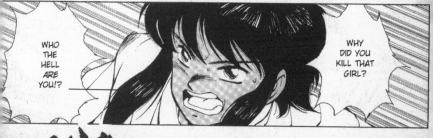

WHO THE HELL ARE YOU!?

WHY DID YOU KILL THAT GIRL?

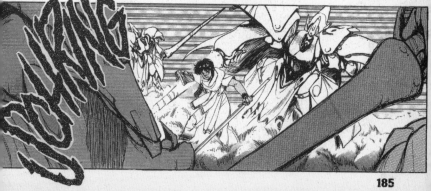

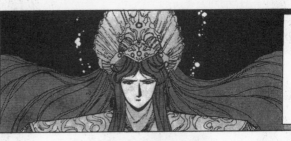

MY NAME IS AIDA. I AM THE FIRST BEING FROM A FAR-OFF PLANET TO VISIT THE SILK ROAD.

I WAS PERSECUTED BY THE HUMANS OF THIS LAND AND WAS CONFINED TO THIS LAKE.

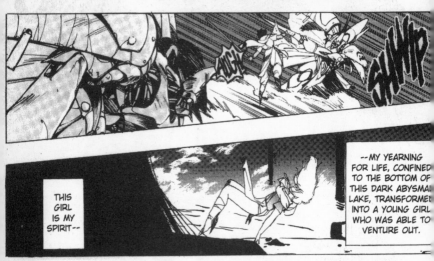

THIS GIRL IS MY SPIRIT--

--MY YEARNING FOR LIFE, CONFINED TO THE BOTTOM OF THIS DARK ABYSMAL LAKE, TRANSFORMED INTO A YOUNG GIRL WHO WAS ABLE TO VENTURE OUT.

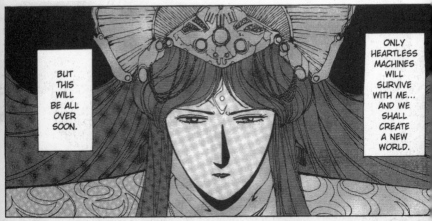

BUT THIS WILL BE ALL OVER SOON.

ONLY HEARTLESS MACHINES WILL SURVIVE WITH ME... AND WE SHALL CREATE A NEW WORLD.

HYAAAA!
!!

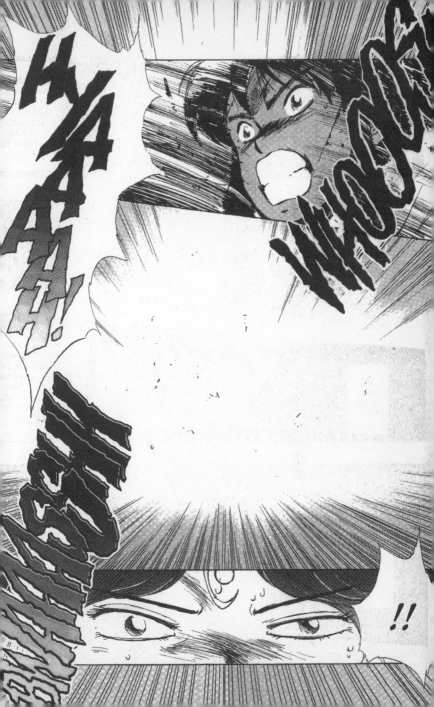

FWOOOOSH
WHAT'S WRONG?
CLANK

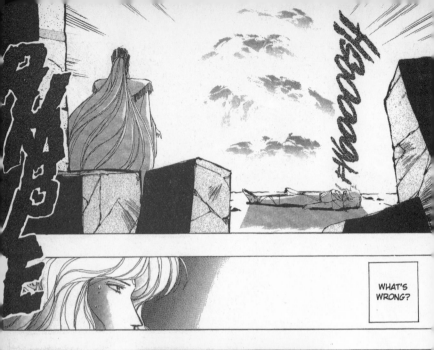

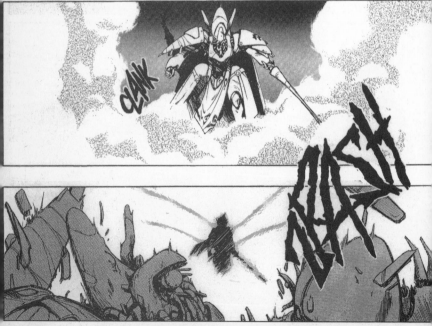

YOU WON'T GET AWAY WITH THIS!!

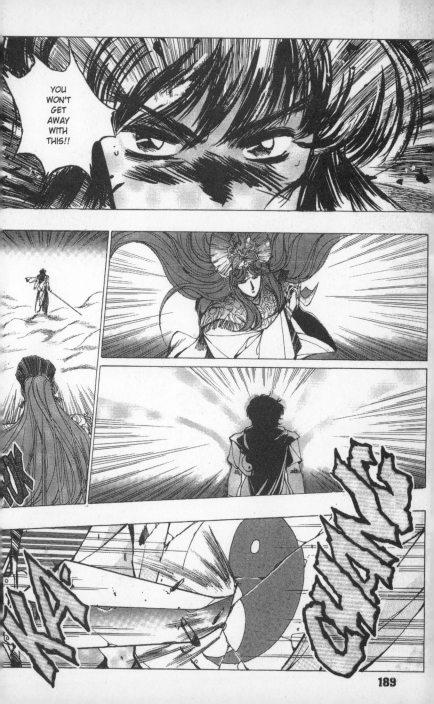

UGGH!
UUHH...
tmp
TH-THUMP
HERE! LET ME HELP YOU DIS-APPEAR!!

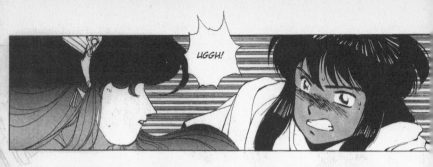

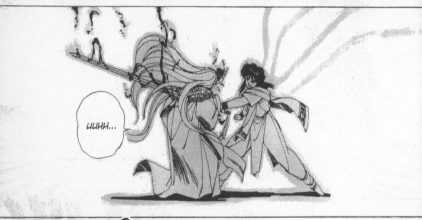

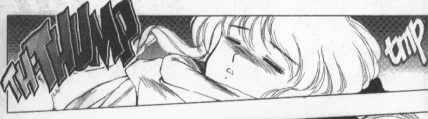

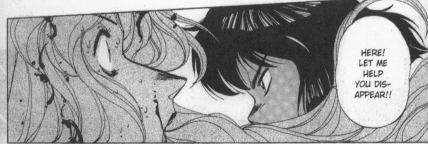

ZWOOOOOOSSH

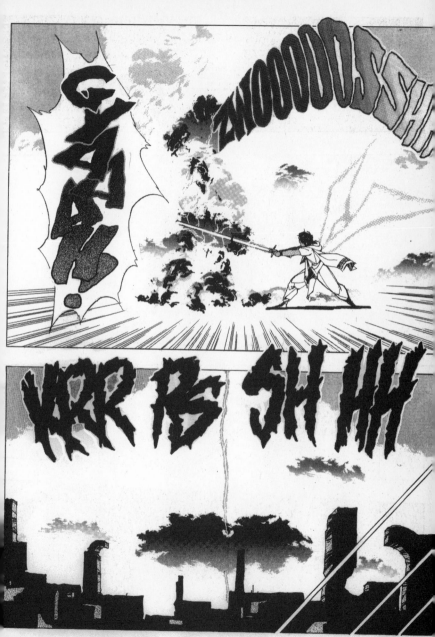

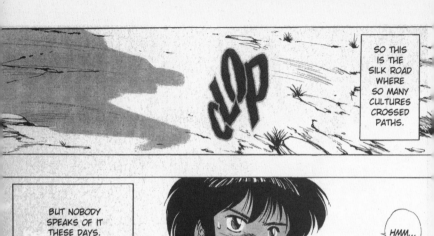

SO THIS IS THE SILK ROAD WHERE SO MANY CULTURES CROSSED PATHS.

BUT NOBODY SPEAKS OF IT THESE DAYS. THERE'S NOTHING BUT GHOSTS HERE NOW!

HMM...

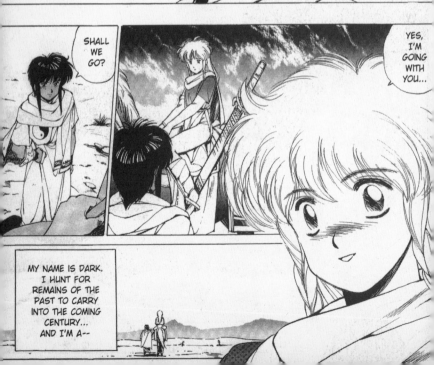

SHALL WE GO?

YES, I'M GOING WITH YOU...

MY NAME IS DARK. I HUNT FOR REMAINS OF THE PAST TO CARRY INTO THE COMING CENTURY... AND I'M A--

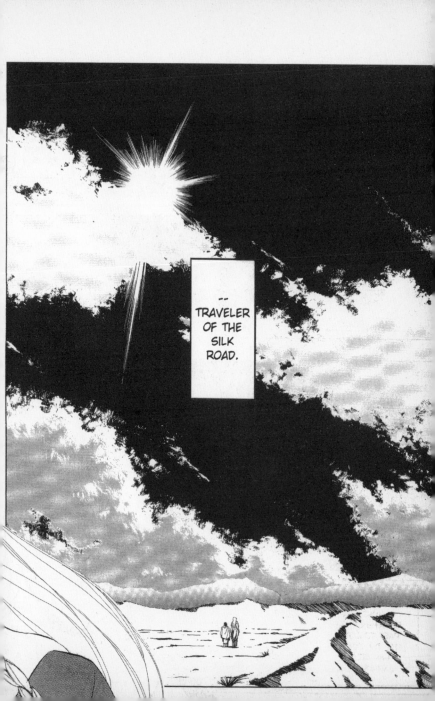

--
TRAVELER
OF THE
SILK
ROAD.

YEAH, THIS IS IT. THIS IS IT.
DARK ANGEL PRODUCTION REPORT.
No.1
THIS IS STUDIO TRON, KIA ASAMIYA'S STUDIO.
IT LOOKS A LOT BIGGER THAN IT DID A FEW YEARS AGO.
Ms. Type '92.
HELLO ...IS ANYONE HERE?
HI, TYPE, WHAT'S UP?
OH, HI!
YOU MUST BE MR. ABE, THE CHIEF.
SWISH
TA DAA!
YEP, I'M SHINOBU ABE, THE CHIEF ART ASSISTANT.

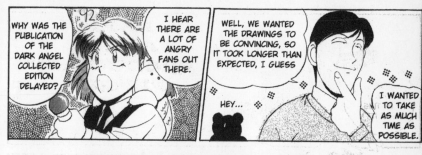

WHY WAS THE PUBLICATION OF THE DARK ANGEL COLLECTED EDITION DELAYED?

I HEAR THERE ARE A LOT OF ANGRY FANS OUT THERE.

WELL, WE WANTED THE DRAWINGS TO BE CONVINCING, SO IT TOOK LONGER THAN EXPECTED, I GUESS

HEY...

I WANTED TO TAKE AS MUCH TIME AS POSSIBLE.

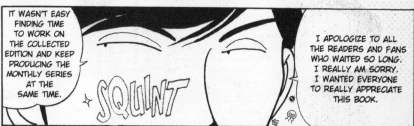

IT WASN'T EASY FINDING TIME TO WORK ON THE COLLECTED EDITION AND KEEP PRODUCING THE MONTHLY SERIES AT THE SAME TIME.

SQUINT

I APOLOGIZE TO ALL THE READERS AND FANS WHO WAITED SO LONG. I REALLY AM SORRY. I WANTED EVERYONE TO REALLY APPRECIATE THIS BOOK.

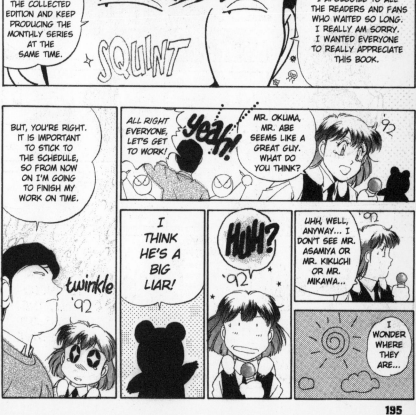

BUT, YOU'RE RIGHT. IT IS IMPORTANT TO STICK TO THE SCHEDULE, SO FROM NOW ON I'M GOING TO FINISH MY WORK ON TIME.

ALL RIGHT EVERYONE, LET'S GET TO WORK!

yeah!

MR. OKUMA, MR. ABE SEEMS LIKE A GREAT GUY. WHAT DO YOU THINK?

twinkle

I THINK HE'S A BIG LIAR!

HUH?

UHH, WELL, ANYWAY... I DON'T SEE MR. ASAMIYA OR MR. KIKUCHI OR MR. MIKAWA...

I WONDER WHERE THEY ARE...

195

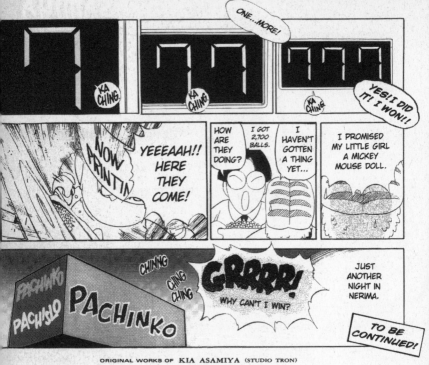

ORIGINAL WORKS OF KIA ASAMIYA (STUDIO TRON)
PUBLISHER TSUGUHIKO KADOKAWA
EDITOR SHINOBU KUWAHARA
SHINICHIRO INOUE
OSAMU OHTA
BOOK DESIGN TETSUYA ASAKURA AND design CREST
ORIGINAL COLOR WORKS KUMIKO NAKAYAMA
TITLE DESIGNED TETSUYA ASAKURA
PRODUCTION MANAGER TOSHIHIKO MIKAWA (STUDIO TRON)
TOTAL ADVISER MICHITAKA KIKUCHI (STUDIO TRON)
CHIEF ART ASSISTANT SHINOBU ABEBE (STUDIO TRON)
REGULAR ART ASSISTANTS HIROTAKA OHKUMA
TAKASHI SAKAI (STUDIO TRON)
TSUTOMU ISOMATA (STADIO TRON)
YUJI KOMATSU
YOSHIAKI NAKAHAMA
TAKAKO ISHIDA (STADIO TORON)
GUEST ART ASSISTANTS MITSUHIRO MORIYAMA
KENJI NITTA
HIROKI SAITO
YUTAKA KARYU
NAOKI MOCHIZUKI
YUUKI SASAKI
YUJI USHIDA
TAKESHI OKAZAKI
O.P. COLOR OBJECT MASAKAZU OHWA (G·G·P)